THE AMAZING MATHEMATICAL AMUSEMENT ARCADE

Brian Bolt

CAMBRIDGE
UNIVERSITY PRESS

Also by this author
The Mathematical Funfair
Mathematical Activities
More Mathematical Activities
Even More Mathematical Activities

PUBLISHED BY THE PRESS SYNDICATE OF THE UNIVERSITY OF CAMBRIDGE
The Pitt Building, Trumpington Street, Cambridge CB2 1RP, United Kingdom

CAMBRIDGE UNIVERSITY PRESS
The Edinburgh Building, Cambridge CB2 2RU, United Kingdom
40 West 20th Street, New York, NY 10011–4211, USA
10 Stamford Road, Oakleigh, Melbourne 3166, Australia

First published 1984
Tenth printing 1998

Printed in the United Kingdom at the University Press, Cambridge

A catalogue record for this book is available from the British Library

ISBN 0 521 269806 paperback

The author and publisher would like to thank The Mansell Collection for permission to reproduce Albert Dürer's *Melancholia*

CONTENTS

Page numbers in bold refer to the amusements; the second page number to the commentary. An asterisk indicates the possible need of a calculator.

INTRODUCTION

Mathematical puzzles are enjoyed by a large number of people of all ages. This collection of puzzles and activities has been selected from a resource book written for teachers which had widespread success. It contains all the creative activities of the earlier book which do not require specific mathematical knowledge, and a significant injection of new ideas. Many of the puzzles have a very long history, others are original, while some rely on the advent of the pocket calculator to be realistically feasible.

The puzzles involve matchsticks, coins, tricky river crossings, and frustrating railway shunting situations. Chessboard puzzles; magic squares, stars and circles; snooker and darts, all find a place. For anyone who has never cut up a Möbius strip then here is your opportunity to be baffled.

The second part of the book is given over to a commentary on the puzzles so that you can check your solution or find a hint when you are stuck. But persevere with your own attempts – it gives a lot of satisfaction to crack a puzzle on your own, and when you have done it, challenge your friends!

Brian Bolt

AMUSEMENTS

1 Matchstick triangles

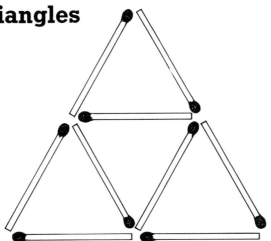

Arrange nine matches to form four small equilateral triangles as shown. Now find a way of arranging only six of the matches to form four triangles of the same shape and size.

2 A tricky river crossing

This is a very old puzzle. It tells of a showman travelling the countryside on tour with a wolf, a goat, and a cabbage. He comes to a river bank and the only means of getting across is a small boat which can hold him with only one of the wolf, the goat or the cabbage.

Unfortunately he dare not leave the wolf alone with the goat or the goat alone with the cabbage for the wolf would eat the goat and the goat would eat the cabbage. After some thought the showman realised that he could use the boat to transport himself and all his belongings safely across the river. How did he do it?

1

3 The baffled engine driver

The diagram shows a circular railway siding at the end of a main line.

C is a cattle truck, S is a sheep truck, E is an engine, and FB is a footbridge over the line.

The problem is to shunt the trucks so that the cattle truck and sheep truck change places and the engine is back on the main line.

The height of the footbridge is such that the engine can pass underneath but the trucks are both too high to do so.

Can you help the engine driver?

4 Make your own dice

Each of the three shapes shown can be folded up to make a dice. In each case three of the numbers are missing. Show how to number the squares correctly so that the number on the opposite faces of the cube add up to 7.

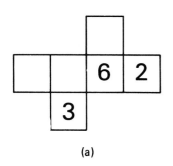

(a)

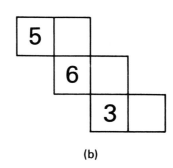

(b)

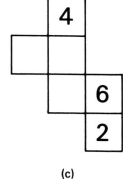

(c)

5 Map folding

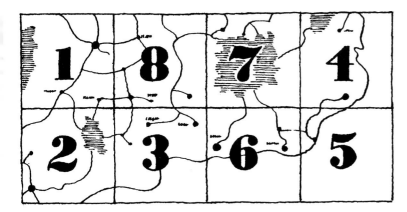

A map is twice as long as it is wide. It can be folded up into
a square, one-eighth the size of the original map, in many ways.
Number the squares as shown on a piece of paper and see
how many ways you can fold it. You can record each way by
noting down the order in which the numbers come next to
each other in the folded map.

The real test of your skill is to fold the map so that the
numbers come in the order 1, 2, 3, 4, 5, 6, 7, 8.

6 The ingenious milkman

A milkman has only a 5 pint jug and a 3 pint jug to measure
out milk for his customers from a milk churn.

How can he measure 1 pint without wasting any milk?

7 Pawns on a chessboard

This is the classical problem of placing sixteen pawns on a chessboard so that no three of the pawns are in line.

It is essentially the same situation as in the previous activity, but with an 8 × 8 board it is not so easy to spot when three pawns are in line.

The diagram shows several lines of pawns which are not at all obvious at first sight namely *ABC*, *ECD* and *FCG*.

When you think you have correctly placed sixteen pawns on an 8 × 8 board so that no three are in a line, get someone else to check your solution before looking at the solution at the back of this book.

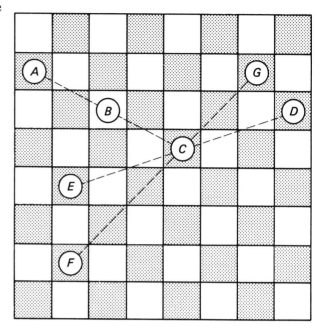

8 Avoid three

This game can be played with pawns or draughts on a chessboard, counters on squared paper, or pegs on a pegboard.

Players take turns to add a piece to the board. A player loses the game when he plays a piece to make a line of three.

Note the game could never exceed seventeen moves because the largest number of pieces which can be placed on an 8 × 8 board without having three in line is sixteen. The skill in the game is to select patterns of play which force your opponent into having to complete a line.

In the diagram there are only twelve pieces on the board but they are so placed that the next person to play will have to make a line of three and thus lose. Check each empty square in turn to convince yourself that this is so. A straight-edge may help.

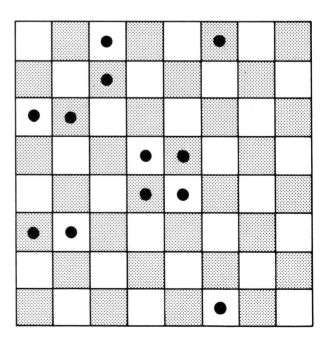

9 Two halves make a whole

Show how to cut the shaded shape A into two pieces which can be rearranged to make any of the shapes $B, C, D, E, F,$ and G.

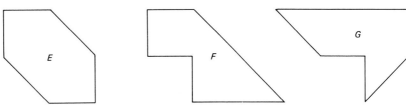

10 Cubism

Some corners are cut out of four wooden cubes.

Afterwards only two of the solids formed are the same shape.

Which two are they?

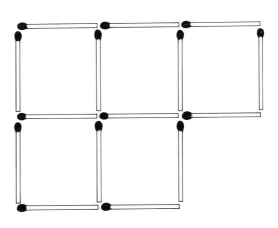

11 Matchstick squares

Remove three matches from the fifteen in the arrangement shown so that only three squares are left.

Now try removing two matches from the arrangement shown to leave three squares. (This time the squares need not all be the same size.)

12 Curves of pursuit

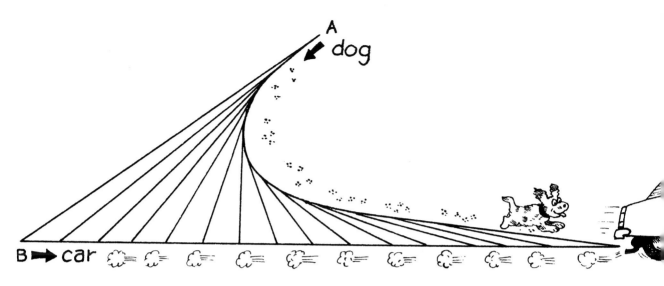

You must have seen, at some time, a dog chase a car or a cyclist. Have you ever considered the path it takes? The dog does not think ahead and run to where the car will be, but usually runs towards the position of the car at that instant.

The drawing above shows the path of a dog which starts running towards a car which it first notices at B. The car is travelling at a constant speed along the line BC and it is assumed that the dog can run at half the speed of the car.

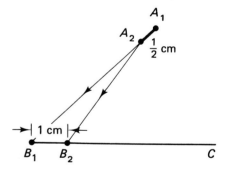

The path can be easily constructed in the following way.

Draw a line B_1C to represent the path of the car. Then take a point A_1 (anywhere will do) to represent the dog's starting position.

Draw a line from A_1 to B_1. This is the direction in which the dog starts to run. Because a dog cannot easily change direction between strides it will run in this direction for a short distance to A_2. This is represented in the drawing by $\frac{1}{2}$ cm.

But while the dog is running from A_1 to A_2 the car has travelled from B_1 to B_2, a distance of 1 cm in the drawing.

At A_2 the dog changes direction towards the car at B_2 and takes a stride in this direction while the car travels to B_3. The process is repeated until the dog's path is found.

Try first to make a drawing more or less like the one shown here. Then experiment with what happens if, for example, the car travels on a circle, or the relative speeds of the dog and car change. The possibilities are endless!

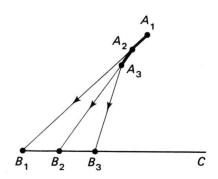

13 The misguided missiles

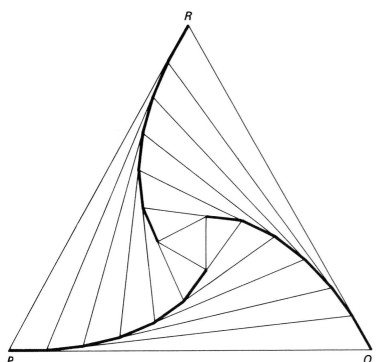

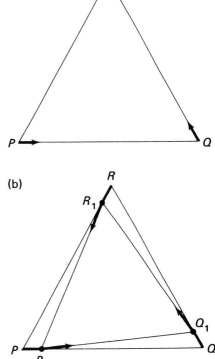

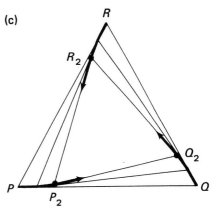

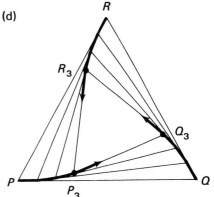

This interesting drawing is another example of finding curves of pursuit. In this case imagine three guided missiles P, Q and R based at three points each 100 km apart at the vertices of an equilateral triangle. The three missiles are all launched at the same time. P homes onto Q, Q homes onto R, and R homes onto P. At regular intervals the missiles change direction to home onto the new position of their targets. The sequence of diagrams (a) to (d) shows how to construct the path of each missile as it chases its neighbour.

Start by drawing an equilateral triangle whose sides are all 10 cm. Mark the points P_1, Q_1, R_1, 1 cm from the points P, Q, R, and draw the triangle $P_1 Q_1 R_1$. Now mark the points P_2, Q_2, R_2, 1 cm from P_1, Q_1, R_1, and draw $P_2 Q_2 R_2$. Continue this process, always marking off along the sides of the last triangle formed, until the missiles explode in the centre!

What would the paths look like if you started with four missiles at the corners of a square?

14 Pattern

Mathematics is all about the analysis and use of pattern. These may be number patterns or geometric patterns. The attractive design here has been formed by fitting together four of the drawings from the previous activity concerned with the pursuit curves of guided missiles. Many other attractive designs can result from the same starting point. All that is required is some patience and careful drawings.

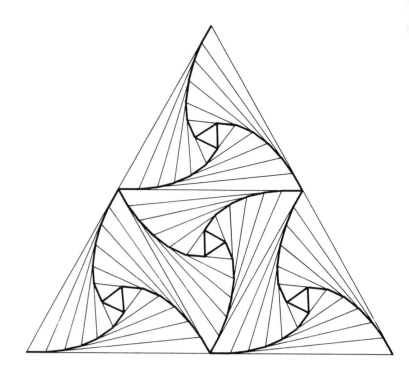

15 The army's predicament

An army on the march through the jungle came to a river which was wide, deep and infested with crocodiles. On the far bank they could see two native boys with a canoe. The canoe can hold one man with his rifle and kit or two boys. How does the army cross the river?

16 The farmer's sheep-pens

This drawing shows how a farmer used thirteen hurdles to make six identical sheep pens. Unfortunately one of the hurdles was damaged.

Use twelve matchsticks to represent the undamaged hurdles and show how the farmer can still make six identical pens.

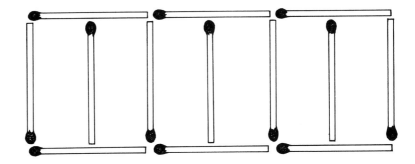

17 The knight's dance

Two white knights and two black knights are placed at the corners of a 3 x 3 square on a chessboard as shown.

How can you make the white knights change places with the black knights in the fewest number of moves?

18 The railway sidings

A railway line BC has two very short sidings BA and CA.
In each siding is a single truck, labelled T_1 and T_2 in the
diagram. On the main line BC is an engine. You have to
decide how to use the engine to shunt the trucks so that
they change places and the engine can return to the main
line. Before trying, however, note that the portion of the
rails at A common to the two sidings is only long enough
for a single truck such as T_1 or T_2, but is too short for
the engine, so that if the engine travels in along CA it cannot come out along AB. Trucks can be linked to each other
or to either end of the engine, but bouncing off the buffers
at A is not allowed!

19 The multi-coloured cube

Imagine you have eight wooden one-centimetre cubes. Show
how they could be painted so that they could be fitted
together to make either a red two-centimetre cube or a blue
two-centimetre cube.

Now consider the similar problem with 27 one-centimetre
cubes. Can you colour the cubes in such a way that they
could be assembled into a red three-centimetre, a blue three-
centimetre cube or a yellow three-centimetre cube?

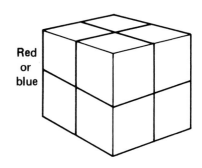

Red
or
blue

20 The jealous husbands

After a flood three married
couples found themselves
surrounded by water, and
had to escape from their
holiday hotel in a boat that
would only hold three persons
at a time. Each husband was
so jealous that he would not
allow his wife to be in the
boat or on either bank with
any other man (or men) unless
he was himself present.

Find a way of getting the
couples across the water to
safety which requires the
smallest number of boat
crossings. Swimming or
helicopters are not allowed!

Now solve the problem if
there are five married couples.

21 The extension lead

A room is 30 ft long, 12 ft wide and 12 ft high. There is a
13 amp power point at A in the middle of an end wall 1 ft
from the floor. An extension lead is required to connect A
with a point B in the middle of the opposite wall but 1 ft
from the ceiling.

For safety the lead must be fastened to the surfaces of
the room and not stretch across the middle. Find the shortest
length of cable needed to do the job. No, the answer is not
42 ft.

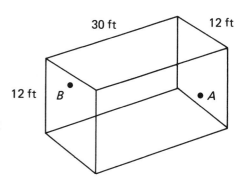

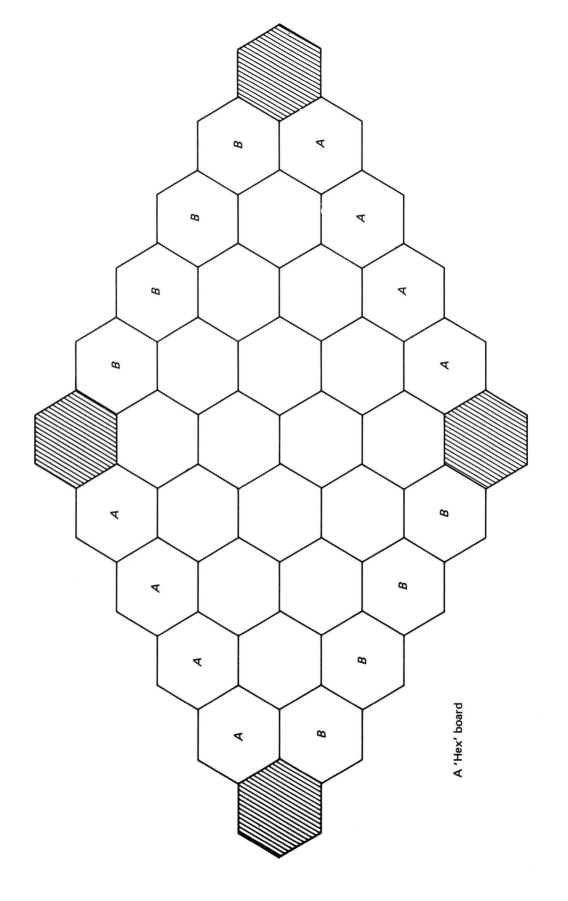

A 'Hex' board

22 Hex

Hex is a board game which was invented in 1942 by Piet Hein, a Danish mathematician. A typical board, shown here, is diamond (rhombus) shaped and is made up of interlocking hexagons. This one has six hexagons on each edge, to start you off, but experts play the game on a board which has eleven hexagons along each edge.

One player has a supply of black counters, the other a supply of white counters. (Any small identifiable objects will do, e.g. buttons, coloured pegs, drawing pins, Smarties.) The players take it in turn to put one of their counters on any unoccupied hexagon. The object of play is to complete a continuous chain of counters from one edge of the board to the opposite edge. 'Black' plays from *A* to *A* while 'white' plays from *B* to *B*. Each player, as well as trying to complete his own chain, naturally tries to block his opponent's attempts.

Drawings (a) and (b) show the results of two games.

Note that the corner hexagons can either be excluded, or counted as being on the edge for both players.

There is more to this game than first appears. Challenge your friends. Have fun, and make yourself a larger board!

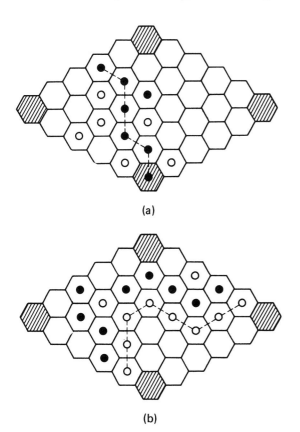

(a)

(b)

23 The square, cross and circle

Three holes are cut in a sheet of metal as shown.

How could one block of wood be cut which could pass through each hole and fit them each exactly?

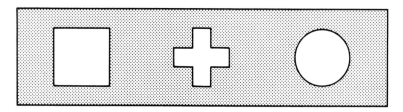

24 The Möbius band

First take a strip of paper *ABCD* about 30 cm long and 2 cm wide and join it in the form of a band as shown in (a). Make the join (sellotape is quick) without twisting the paper so that *A* meets *D* and *B* meets *C*.

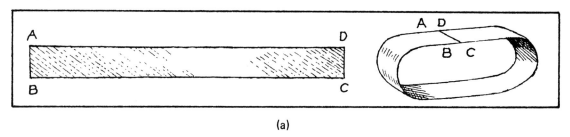

(a)

This band has two easily recognisable surfaces – colour the inside surface.

How many edges has the band?

What would happen to the band if you made a cut right along its length as shown in (b)?

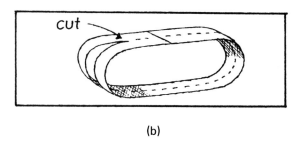

(b)

The answers to the questions so far have all been straightforward, but what follows will certainly surprise you if you have not met it before.

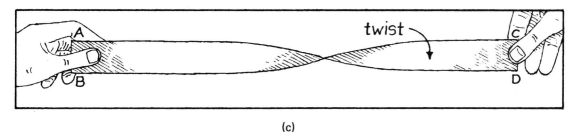

(c)

Start with another strip of paper *ABCD*. Now twist one end of the strip through 180° before joining it into a band with *A* meeting *C* and *B* meeting *D,* as shown in (d).

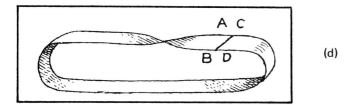

(d)

This new style band is known as a Möbius band and has many fascinating properties.

Try colouring the 'inside' of the band and you will find it only has one side. This fact is used by engineers in belts connecting pulleys. By making the belt a Möbius band the engineer ensures it will wear evenly.

How many edges has the band?

Now for another surprise! Cut along the length of the band along its middle until you come to the starting point.

What do you find?

Now make another Möbius band and cut along it, always keeping a third of the distance from the edge (see (e)). After cutting twice around the band you should come back to the starting point.

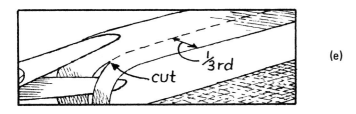

(e)

What is the result this time? Did you predict it? Experiment with bands having more twists.

See if you can come to any general conclusions.

25 The economical gardener

A gardener liked to make the most of the plants she had and one day she found, when laying out a rose bed, that she had managed to plant seven rose bushes in such a way that they formed six lines with three rose bushes in each line. How did she do it?

Pleased with herself the gardener looked for other interesting arrangements until she found a way of planting ten rose bushes so that she had five lines with four rose bushes in each line.

Find her arrangements.

Investigate other 'economic' arrangements.

26 How many triangles can you see?

The figure contains many triangles, some of which overlap each other.

Make a copy of the diagram and find a systematic way of accounting for all the triangles.

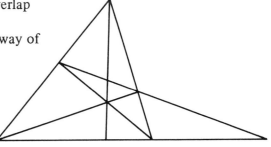

27 The unfriendly power-boats

Two radio-controlled power-boats are moored 200 metres apart at A and B near the centre of a large lake. The boats are both controlled by the same radio transmitter in such a way that they move at the same speed. However, the boat which leaves B has a faulty steering mechanism and moves on a bearing which is always 90° more than the bearing of the boat which leaves A. How can the controller steer the boats to meet each other?

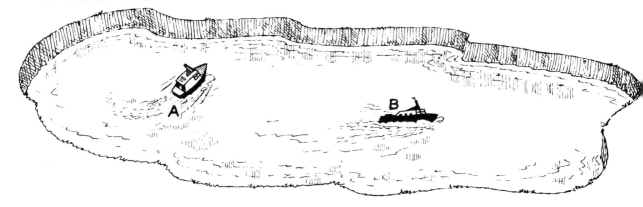

28 The knight-guards

Show how to place twelve
knights on a chessboard so
that every square is either
occupied or attacked.

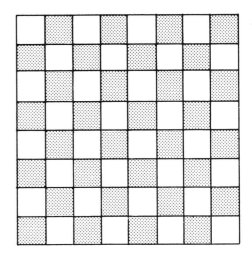

29 Reversing the trains

The diagram shows the plan
of the rail network in a large
town. Each small circle is a
station and each number refers
to a train. The station at the
bottom has no train.

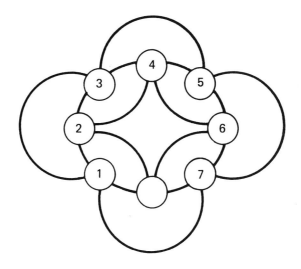

By moving one train at a time to the station left empty,
show how to move the trains so that their order is reversed.
That is, 1 is in the position of 7, 2 in the position of 6 and
so on.

The first move must be made by either 1, 2, 7 or 6.

The reversal of the trains' order can be made in as few as
fifteen moves.

30 Quadruplets

Show how the shape on the
right can be divided into
four pieces which are identical
to each other.

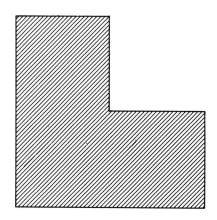

31 Complete the square

Carefully draw the five shapes
shown here on squared paper.
Cut them out and then show
how they can be put together
to form a square. Do not
despair – it is possible!

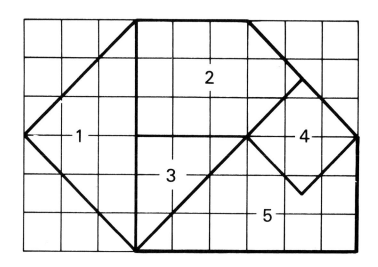

32 Roll a penny

A penny *A* is rolled around a
second penny *B* without
slipping until it returns to its
starting point.

How many revolutions
does penny *A* make?

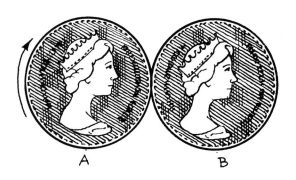

33 The growing network

This is a game for two players sometimes known as 'Sprouts'.
All that is required is a piece of paper and a pencil. Mark
three points anywhere on the paper, as in (a).

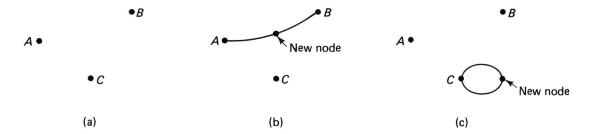

(a)　　　　　　　　　(b)　　　　　　　　　(c)

These points will become nodes of a network as the game
progresses. The first player joins any two points by an arc
and then makes a new point (node) in the middle of this arc,
as in (b). Alternatively the player may draw an arc which
starts and ends at the same point, but again he must add a
new node in the middle of the arc, as in (c).

The next player then adds a new arc to the network and
a new node in the middle of his arc. He may join his arc to
any node(s) as long as the node(s) he uses do not end up
with more than three branches.

As soon as a node has three branches it is 'out of bounds'
and can be circled to indicate this.

The drawings in (d) show just some of the possible moves
for the second player if the first player joined *A* to *B*.

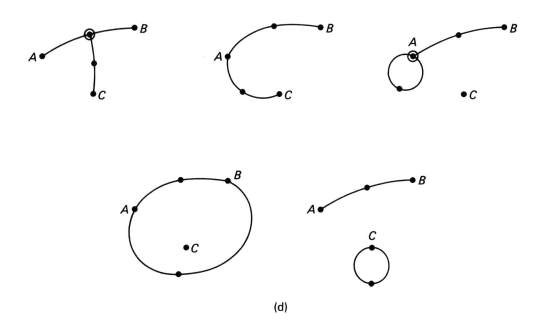

(d)

The object of the game is to prevent your opponent from being able to make a move. The last player to draw in a legitimate arc wins. One further rule: arcs may not cross over other arcs.

It pays to remember this rule, for nodes may get cut off and become unusable even though they do not have three branches.

Diagram (e) shows the network produced by one game. Although at this stage there are two nodes, X and Y, which do not have three branches, they cannot be joined.

Play this game with your friends and then try the following.

(i) Try to explain why the game must end after a limited number of moves. (How many?)
(ii) Try starting with four or five points.
(iii) Investigate the effect of having 4–nodes (i.e. nodes which have *four* branches) instead of 3–nodes.

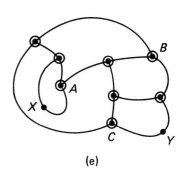

(e)

34 Traversibility

Drawing (a) is a map of a road network. A road engineer starting at A wants to travel along each road once only and return to A. How can he do it?

Network (b) cannot be traced out with a pencil unless you go over some lines twice or take your pencil off the paper and start at another point.

Find the smallest number of times you need to take your pencil off the paper to draw it.

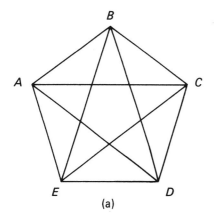

(a)

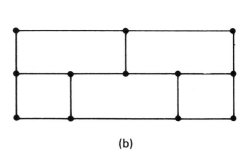

(b)

35 Impossible rotations!

Katy challenged her friends to take a book, rotate it through an angle of 180° and then rotate it again through 180° so that the book ends up at 90° to its original position. How can it be done?

36 The hunter

A hunter followed his prey 3 miles south, 3 miles east and then eventually shot it after stalking it for another 3 miles which took him back to the point where he started.

   What was his prey?

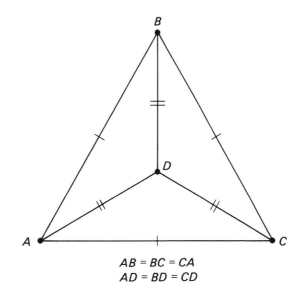

37 Four points in a plane

Mark four points on a flat surface so that there are only two different distances between them.

   One arrangement is shown. There are five other possible arrangements. Find them!

$$AB = BC = CA$$
$$AD = BD = CD$$

38 The letter dice

A word game uses dice with a letter on each face. Three views of one of the dice are shown above. Which letter is on the face opposite H?

39 The queen's defence

What is the smallest number of queens which can be put on an $n \times n$ chessboard so as to occupy or command all the squares on a board?

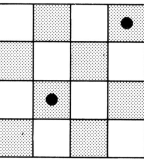

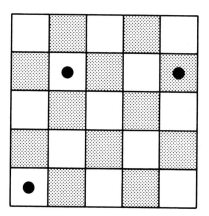

Here is a solution for the 4 x 4 board with two queens and a solution for the 5 x 5 boards with three queens.

Find other solutions for the 4 x 4 and 5 x 5 boards and then find a solution for the 6 x 6 board with three queens.

How many queens are needed when $n = 7$ and $n = 8$?

In 1862 Jaenisch proposed a variation on this problem in which not only were all squares to be occupied or commanded, but no queen was to be on a square which was under attack by another.

A related problem would be to find the smallest number of queens which would occupy or command every square subject to the restriction that every queen was protected by another.

Clearly similar problems could be set for the other chess pieces.

40 Seeing is believing

Cut out the shapes drawn on the 8 × 8 square and rearrange
to form the 13 × 5 rectangle.

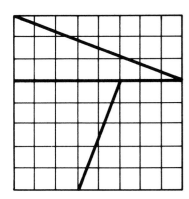

This means   64 = 65.   Where is the catch?

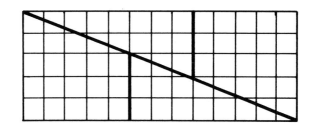

41 Inspecting the roads

The plan shows the road network connecting nine villages.
The numbers refer to the
mileages along the roads.

A council workman living
at village *A* wants to inspect
all the roads in a car. What
is the shortest route he can
take if he has to return to *A*?

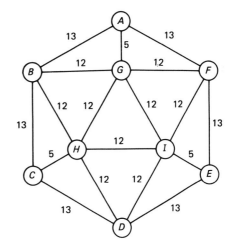

42 Dominoes on a chessboard

A domino is the same shape
and size as two squares on a
chessboard.

It is easy to see how to
place 32 such dominoes on
a chessboard so as to cover
it.

Can you decide however
if it is possible to cover the
board shown here, with the
squares at two opposite
corners missing, with 31 such
dominoes?

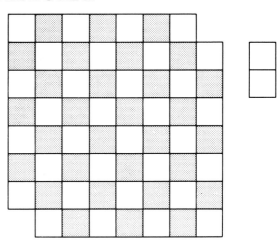

43 Zigzag

Use a 7 x 7 or 9 x 9 square
array of dots.

Start at the centre dot, *S*.

The first player draws an
arrow either across or up and
down to the nearest dot.

The second player follows
with an arrow to form a
continuous path.

The players move alter-
nately. The object is to form
a path from *S* to the home
base (*A* for the first player, *B*
for the second player) without
visiting any point more than
once. The first player to home
base wins.

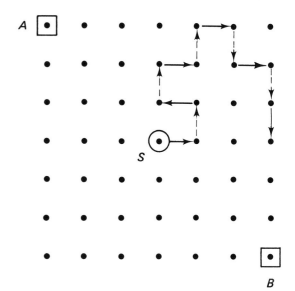

44 Knight's tours

One of the classical problems in recreational mathematics
is to investigate paths on a chessboard which a knight can
follow in such a way that it visits every square on the board
once and only once. Many famous mathematicians such as
De Moivre, Euler and Vandermonde have written about this
problem over the last 200 years but there is always some-
thing new to be found.

One solution due to De Moivre for the 8 x 8 board is indicated in (a) where the squares are numbered to indicate the
knight's progress. In (b) is shown an alternative way of representing the same path. They both have their merits and you
can decide which is the more appropriate for your investi-
gations. (You will need a plentiful supply of squared paper
however if you are to make any progress whichever method
you use.) The second method using lines to connect the
squares has not been completed but it already shows the
strategy of De Moivre's solution which was essentially to
move round the board in one direction always keeping as
close to the outer boundary as possible. Copy diagram (b)
onto squared paper and complete De Moivre's solution
before trying one of your own.

34	49	22	11	36	39	24	1
21	10	35	50	23	12	37	40
48	33	62	57	38	25	2	13
9	20	51	54	63	60	41	26
32	47	58	61	56	53	14	3
19	8	55	52	59	64	27	42
46	31	6	17	44	29	4	15
7	18	45	30	5	16	43	28

(a)

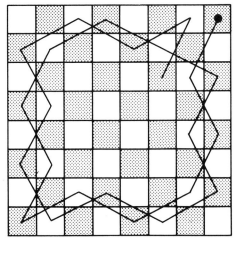

(b)

In a problem like this it is often helpful to start with a smaller board to get a feel for the way in which a knight can move to the other squares around it on a board.

On a 3 x 3 board it is soon clear that a knight's tour of the whole board is impossible. Either the knight starts on an outside square when it can easily visit all the outer squares but not the middle square, or it starts in the middle when no move is possible.

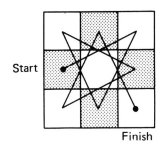

(c)

Is it possible to find a knight's tour on a 4 x 4 board? Diagram (d) shows a false trail which ran out of moves after the fourth. If you cannot achieve all sixteen squares, what is the largest number which you can visit without retracing your steps?

Investigate paths on 5 x 5, 6 x 6 and 7 x 7 boards.

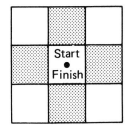

(d)

25

Diagram (e) shows a knight's tour on an 8 x 4 rectangular board.

Is it possible to find a knight's tour on a smaller rectangular board?

18	13	32	9	28	5	22	1
31	10	19	16	21	2	25	6
14	17	12	29	8	27	4	23
11	30	15	20	3	24	7	26

(e)

It is interesting to investigate other shapes which can be toured by a knight. The shape in diagram (f) can be, although the author had convinced himself it was not possible when he first investigated it!

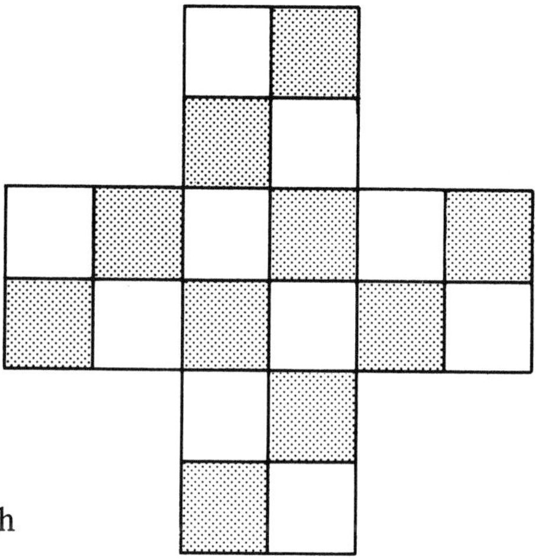

(f)

However, to return to the classical problem on a square board, the mathematicians who investigated it tried to find solutions with special properties. One type of solution was to find a knight's tour which ended a knight's move from the starting square. A solution of this type due to Euler is shown below. Such a solution is said to form a re-entrant path. The solution shown in (g) has a further intriguing property in that one half of the board is completed before the other half is entered.

58	43	60	37	52	41	62	35
49	46	57	42	61	36	53	40
44	59	48	51	38	55	34	63
47	50	45	56	33	64	39	54
22	7	32	1	24	13	18	15
31	2	23	6	19	16	27	12
8	21	4	29	10	25	14	17
3	30	9	20	5	28	11	26

(g) Euler's re-entrant half-board solution

1	48	31	50	33	16	63	18
30	51	46	3	62	19	14	35
47	2	49	32	15	34	17	64
52	29	4	45	20	61	36	13
5	44	25	56	9	40	21	60
28	53	8	41	24	57	12	37
43	6	55	26	39	10	59	22
54	27	42	7	58	23	38	11

(h) Euler's magic square solution

Try to find a re-entrant path on a 6 × 6 board.

There is a neat proof to show that a re-entrant path on any board having an odd number of squares is impossible. See if you can find the reason.

Re-entrant paths are possible on a variety of shapes. Try this one (i).

Another clever solution due to Euler which defeated many other seekers was that of a knight's tour whose squares when numbered in the usual fashion formed an 8 × 8 magic square (i.e. the sums of the numbers in any row or column, but not diagonal, add up to the same total, in this case 260). This square is given in (h). Check its 'magic' property and investigate the symmetry of its path.

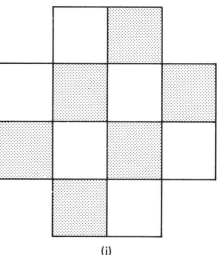

An interesting game of strategy for two players based on a knight's tour can be played as follows. Start on any square of a 5 × 5 board and produce a knight's path by players taking in turn to make a knight's move from the last position reached. The move must not land on a square previously used and the winner is the last player able to move.

(i)

45 Sawing up a cube

A 3 cm wooden cube is to be sawn into 27 one-centimetre cubes. Is it possible to achieve this with fewer than six saw cuts?

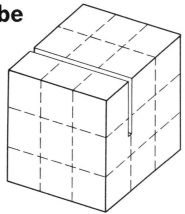

46 The improbable hole

Improbable though it may seem, it is possible to cut a hole through a solid cube so that a cube, larger than the original, can be passed in one end and out the other.

How do you cut the hole?

47 Identical twins

Divide shapes X and Y into two equal pieces.

Make a similar puzzle yourself.

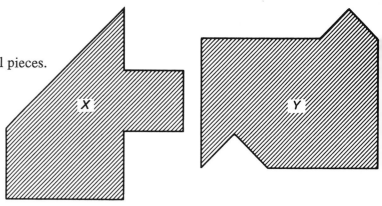

48 The four-colour theorem

How many colours are needed to colour a map so that any regions which have part of their boundary in common must be of a different colour? (Two regions with a point in common may be the same colour.)

The map shown here appears to require five colours as it has been shaded but it can be coloured in using only four colours. How?

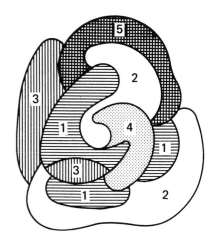

For as long as map making has been practised the map makers have believed that the different regions on a map could always be coloured using only four colours. Mathematicians have been trying to prove this result since Möbius mentioned it in a lecture in 1840. However, it defied proof until in 1978 two American mathematicians used a powerful computer to analyse the situation. But many people still have a sneaking feeling that someone will turn up with a map which cannot be coloured with as few as four colours . . . can you find one?

49 Mystifying matchsticks

Take away four matchsticks to leave exactly four equilateral triangles all of the same size.

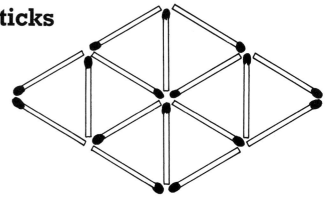

50 Equilateral triangle to square

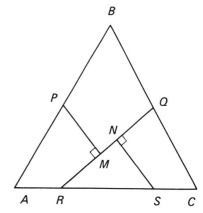

Construct an equilateral triangle ABC then divide it into the four pieces shown where

$$AP = BP, \quad CQ = BQ, \quad AR = \tfrac{1}{4}AC, \quad CS = \tfrac{1}{4}CA$$

and PM and SN are at right angles to RQ. 8 cm is a good length to use for AC.

  Cut the pieces out of card (or for a more permanent puzzle use plywood or hardboard) and then rearrange them to form a square.

51 Squaring the urn

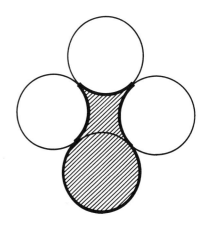

The cross-section of an urn is shown here shaded. It is composed of parts of four circles of the same size as indicated.

  Show how, with two straight cuts, this shape can be divided into three pieces which can be rearranged to make a square.

52 The baffled housewife

Mrs Smith often walked to the bus-stop on the main road to catch a bus into the shopping centre. She didn't ever bother with timetables because it was a busy route and she could catch either a P bus or a Q bus. She knew that there were six buses an hour of each kind so she never had long to wait. What did surprise her, however, was that she hardly ever seemed to travel on a Q bus. She decided to keep a regular check on the kind of bus she caught and found that she only travelled on a Q bus on one ride in ten.

  She was baffled! Can you help her?

29

53 Invert the triangle

A triangle of pennies is made as in (a). What is the smallest number of pennies which have to be moved to turn the triangle pattern upside down as in (b)?

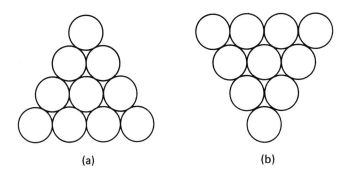

(a)   (b)

54 Avoid that snooker

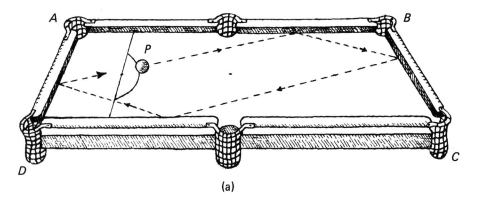

(a)

When a ball P is struck by a cue towards the side cushion of a snooker table it bounces off as if the cushion is a mirror. A typical path of a ball which is first hit towards the side cushion AB is shown in diagram (a). Always supposing there is no ball in its path the ball will then be 'reflected' off the end cushion BC followed by the side cushion CD etc. as shown until it comes to rest.

In the game of snooker the problem is often to strike the cue ball P to make contact with a particular coloured ball which has been purposely snookered (hidden) behind other balls by one's opponent. If any other ball is hit then points are lost so the skill of the game is to learn how to use the side walls of the table to bounce the cue ball onto the target ball.

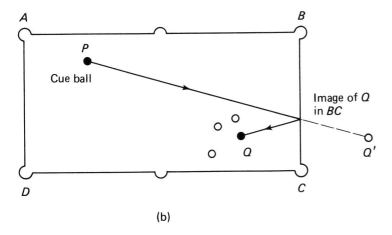

(b)

Diagram (b) represents a situation where Q, the target ball, is snookered by three other balls. In this case the cue ball can be bounced off the end cushion BC. To decide where the cue ball must strike BC, mark in Q' the mirror image of Q in BC, and hit the cue ball towards Q'. The cue ball will then automatically 'reflect' off BC towards Q.

This method can be neatly extended to get out of trickier situations (at least in theory!) where the ball is bounced off two or more cushions. Diagram (c) shows how the cue ball çan be struck to bounce off AB, then off BC before hitting the target ball T.

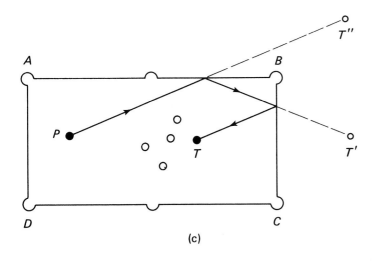

(c)

Because the cue ball is to bounce off BC towards T, it must travel towards BC in the direction of T', where T' is the mirror image of T in BC. To do this it must travel towards AB in the direction of T'', where T'' is the mirror image of T' in AB.

Find where to hit the cue ball P to make contact with
the target ball T in the following situations.

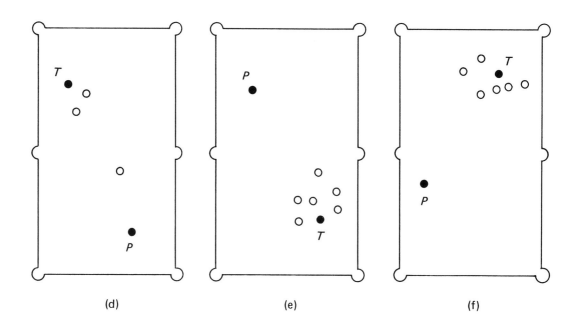

(d) (e) (f)

55 Squares (a game for two players)

This is another version of
noughts and crosses which can
be played on squared paper.
Mark off a board which is a
6 x 6 square or larger.

Players mark noughts and
crosses alternately and the
winner is the first player to
make four of his marks at
the vertices of a square. In
the game shown the player
marking noughts has won.

How many ways of making a square on a 6 x 6 board are
there?

Another version of the game is to play until the board has
been filled with marks and then assess which player has the
larger number of squares.

Yet another alternative is to play to avoid making squares.
The loser is then the first player to form a square.

56 The hungry bookworm

A bookworm started eating its way through a five-volume set
of encyclopaedias starting at the front cover of volume I and
ate its way through to the outside of the back cover of volume
V. If each volume was 3 cm thick how far had the bookworm
travelled? (You may assume the volumes are stacked in
numerical order.)

57 Place the motorway junction

Building roads can be very expensive so civil engineers try to
make them as short as possible. The line of a new motorway
as it passes by the small towns of Green Glades and Pleasant
Pastures is to be as straight as a ruler. It is proposed to make
one junction on the motorway for the local inhabitants and
join it to the towns by straight roads as shown. Where should
the junction be positioned to minimise the total length of the
road G to J to P?

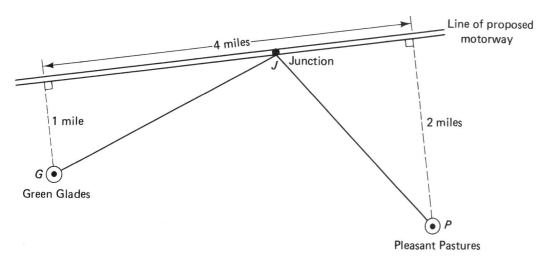

58 Space filling

A unit cube can be fitted together with seven other identical cubes to make a larger cube with an edge of 2 units. How many unit cubes are needed to make a cube with an edge of 3 units?

Given a supply of identical regular tetrahedra (i.e. triangular pyramids whose faces are all equilateral triangles) can you fit them together to make a larger tetrahedron, and if so how many would you need?

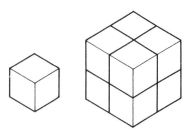 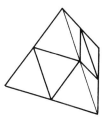

59 Curves from intersecting circles

Many interesting curves and patterns can be found by drawing sets of intersecting circles. Two of these are shown here to give you a start.

In the first example two sets of circles are drawn from two centres A and B. Here the original drawing was made with the distance $AB = 12$ cm and the circles increasing in radius by 1 cm at a time. A set of circles all drawn with the same centre and looking like the ripples formed when a pebble is dropped into a pool are called concentric. When two concentric sets of circles are drawn as below with the circles equally spaced then their intersections lie on sets of ellipses. Four of the ellipses have been drawn in. The ringed numbers give a clue to why the ellipses are formed. For the ellipse labelled 20 you will find that for every point P on it $AP + BP = 20$.

This is easily checked. Take, for example, the point which is on the eighth circle from A and you will find that it is on the twelfth circle from B.

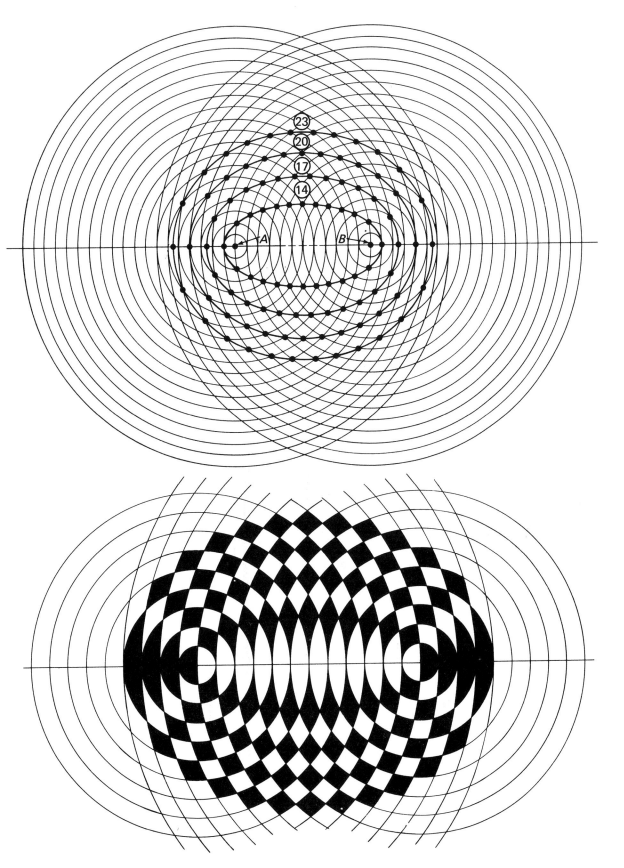

35

Try marking in the ellipses corresponding to 18 and 26. If you have access to a photocopier then it is a good idea to draw two sets of intersecting concentric circles and make several copies of them before marking in the ellipses. Above can be seen the way in which shading in the alternate regions in a chessboard fashion can also highlight the ellipses and make an attractive pattern into the bargain.

Can you see another family of curves in this diagram?

The second example is shown on the right. The curve which appears as the boundary of all the circles is known as a *cardioid*.

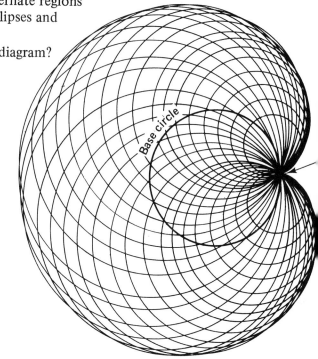

To produce this diagram start with a base circle and mark a point A on it. All the other circles are formed by taking different points on the circumference of the circle and adjusting the radius so that the circles go through A.

Draw as many circles as you want to get the boundary clearly.

What will happen if you start with the point A not on the circumference of the base circle?

60   A lover's ultimatum!

I ask you, sir, to plant a grove
To show that I'm your lady love.
This grove though small must be composed
Of twenty-five trees in twelve straight rows.
In each row five trees you must place
Or you shall never see my face.

61   Only four lines

• • •

• • •   Without taking your pencil from the paper,
                  draw four straight lines that together
• • •   pass through all nine points.

62 How fast can you cycle?

In a time trial a cyclist wanted to average 40 km per hour between two towns A and C which are 10 kilometres apart. A village B is sited exactly halfway between A and C and is reached after a long climb up from A. When the cyclist had climbed up to B she calculated that her average speed so far was only 20 km per hour. How fast must she ride on the descent from B to C if she is to attain the overall average speed of 40 km per hour?

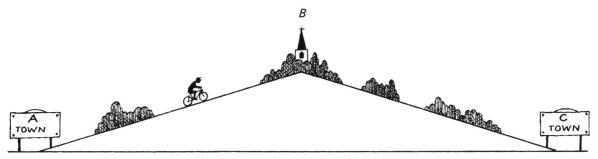

63 The bob-sleigh run

It is proposed to design a new bob-sleigh run at a well-known ski resort. The run is to start at the summit of a hill, S, near the ski lift and end 500 m lower in the village V. No expense is to be spared to build the run to make the descent as fast as possible. What line should the path take from S to V to achieve this?

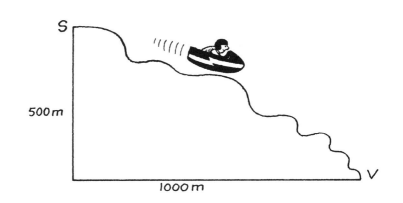

64 Know your vowels

This table contains each of the five vowels – A, E, I, O, U – five times, Show how to cut the 5 x 5 square into five different pieces each of which contains all the vowels once only.

When you have solved this one try making a similar one for yourself.

E	A	I	O	I
U	E	U	E	O
O	I	A	O	A
I	U	E	A	I
A	O	U	E	U

65 Games on a pegboard for one to play

A piece of pegboard (hardboard with holes in) and some coloured pegs is all you need to spend hours happily playing the following solitaire games. Alternatively you could use counters or pawns on a chessboard.

Leapfrog

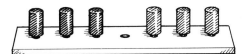

The first game requires a line of seven holes, three pegs of one colour (say black) and three pegs of a second colour (say red). Place them as shown with an empty hole between them. A move consists of (i) moving a peg into the next position if the hole is empty, or (ii) jumping over one piece to an empty hole beyond like a capturing move in draughts.

   The two kinds of move are illustrated below and follow in turn from the starting position.

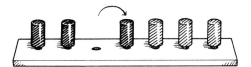
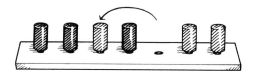

   The object of the game is to find the smallest number of moves to interchange the black pegs and the red pegs.

   Vary the game by having different numbers of pegs at each end and see if you can find a formula for the number of moves required for x black pegs and y red pegs to change ends.

All change!

The second game is very similar to the first game but played on a square board. A 5 × 5 board is shown here with the starting position. There are twelve black pegs, twelve red pegs and an empty hole in the middle.

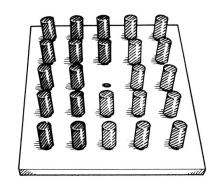

   Moves are as in 'Leapfrog' but now the pegs can be moved from left to right or up and down. No diagonal moves are allowed.

   Show how to interchange the two sets of pegs in 48 moves.

Solitaire

The third game has a very long history and is played across the world. It is available in a commercial form from cheap plastic versions to expensive ones in wood with coloured marbles for the pieces. However pegboard and coloured pegs make a suitable alternative.

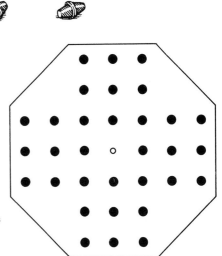

In this game the board has 33 holes arranged in a cross as shown here. There are 32 pegs all of the same colour and they are initially arranged as shown leaving the central hole empty.

This time the only allowable move is to jump over an adjacent peg to an empty hole beyond. The peg which has been jumped over is removed from the board. Only across and up and down moves are allowed and the object is to remove all but one of the pegs.

There are many solutions but the best are considered to be those which end with the last peg in the centre.

Have a go!

There are several traditional problems on a solitaire board where the player has to try to end with a peg in the centre. Here are three of them.

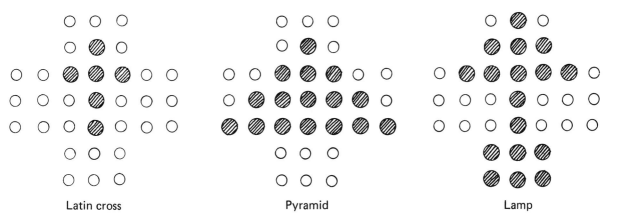

Latin cross   Pyramid   Lamp

66 Two of a kind

Shapes *P* and *Q* can each be divided into two identical pieces. They have been designed on the same principle so that when you have found the solution to one shape the other's solution should soon follow.

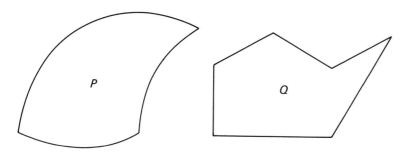

67 Colouring a cube

What is the smallest number of colours needed to paint a cube so that no two adjacent faces are the same?

How many distinctly different cubes can be obtained if four colours are used?

(A face can only be one colour and adjacent faces must be different colours.)

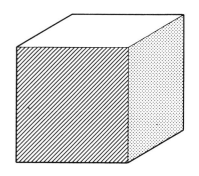

68 Problems of single line working

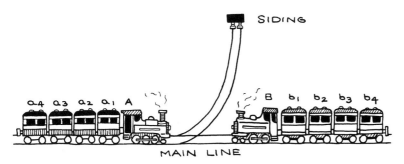

Two passenger trains each with four carriages face each other on a main line. Adjoining the main line is a siding. Unfortunately the siding is only long enough to take an engine and two carriages. Find the most efficient way of shunting the carriages to enable the trains to continue their journey.

69 Two at a time

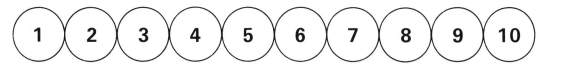

Put ten coins in a line as shown. A move consists of picking up a coin, leaping over two coins and landing on another coin. Show that in five moves it is possible to arrange the coins into five pairs equally spaced. Not as easy as it seems!

70 Heads and tails

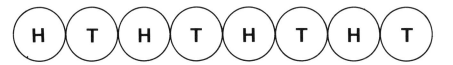

Take eight pennies and place them alternately head and tail touching each other in a line as shown. A move consists of moving two touching pennies to one end or to a suitable space of the row without changing their order.

Show that in four moves it is possible to arrange them in the order T T T T H H H H with the coins touching and in line.

71 Square a Greek cross

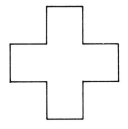

Cut out a Greek cross from a piece of card. Now divide the cross into four pieces with two straight cuts in such a way that the pieces can be rearranged to form a square.

72 The fuel delivery

A large modern city was built with a system of ring roads and link roads as shown. At each of these road junctions the Monopoly Oil Company had a petrol station.

Show that a petrol delivery driver can leave the depot with a tanker and visit each petrol station once and, without passing it again, return to the depot.

Petrol depot

73 Fair shares

A farmer and his friend bought an 8 gallon barrel of cider. They wanted to share the cider equally between them but only had a 5 gallon container and a 3 gallon container. How did they manage?

74 Coin magic

○ ○ ○

○ ○

○ ○ ○

Arrange eight coins as shown to form a square with three coins on each side.

Now move four of the coins to form a square with four coins on each side!

75 The persistent frog

In its search for water a frog fell down a 30 ft well. Its progress out of the well was very erratic. Each day it managed to climb up 3 ft, but the following night it slipped back 2 ft.

How many days did it take the frog to get out of the well?

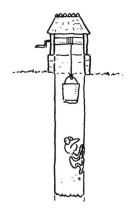

76 Tidy that bookshelf!

Tidying up the order of books on a library bookshelf is a tedious job so the librarian was always concerned to do it in the most efficient way. She found that the best way to arrive at the order she wanted was by a process of interchanging two books at a time. That is, she would remove any two books from the shelf and replace them in the reverse order.

How many interchanges would she require to place the set of encyclopaedias shown in the order 1 2 3 4 5 6 7 8 9?

What would be the most efficient way if the books had been in the order 4 5 7 6 8 1 9 2 3?

Devise a strategy to find which interchanges to make for an optimum solution for tidying up the encyclopaedias no matter how they were left.

77 Cutting up a circle

This sequence of diagrams shows what happens when a number of points are taken on the circumference of a circle and all the chords joining the points are drawn in. If you took a pair of scissors and cut along all the lines in each case the circle will be cut into 2, 4, 8, 16 pieces.

How many pieces will the circle end up as if you do the same with six points on the circumference?

Do not jump to conclusions!

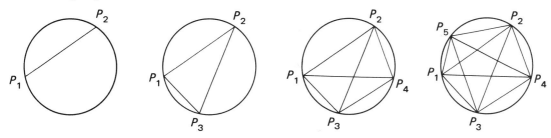

78 Square relations

The number 24 has the property that it is one short of a square number, and its double is also one short of a square number.

$$24 + 1 = 25 = 5^2$$
$$(24 \times 2) + 1 = 49 = 7^2$$

What is the next number with the same property?

79 The numerate gardener

A gardener had a number of equal square paving slabs which he arranged to form two larger square patios of about the same size as each other. Being a dab-hand with figures he realised that with the same number of paving slabs he could have produced two square patios but this time with one much larger than the other. How many paving slabs did the gardener have?

80 Magic triangles

The numbers 1, 2, 3, 4, 5, 6 have been arranged in a triangle so that the sum of the numbers along each side is always the same, 10. Show that the same numbers can be put on the triangle in a different way so that the totals along each side are still constant but equal to another number. There are three possibilities apart from the one shown. Numbers arranged to form a triangle like this are called magic.

Now try arranging the following sets of numbers to form magic triangles:

    (i) 1 2 3 5 6 7
    (ii) 1 2 3 4 6 7

There are two different arrangements in each case.

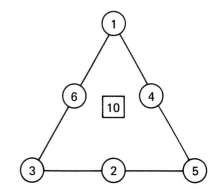

81 Number patterns

There are many fascinating number patterns to investigate.
Here are a few to start you thinking.

1 Choose a digit. Suppose you choose 5. Multiply 5 by 9 to
obtain 45. Now work out

$$12\,345\,679 \times 45$$

Are you surprised at the answer?
   Try another digit such as 3, multiply 3 by 9 to obtain
27 and then work out

$$12\,345\,679 \times 27$$

Can you explain the answer?

2 This is similar to the above. Choose a digit, for example 2,
multiply 2 by 7 to obtain 14, then work out

$$15\,873 \times 14$$

Investigate other digits and explain the results.

3 Complete the following and explain the pattern.

$$143 \times 2 \times 7 =$$
$$143 \times 3 \times 7 =$$
$$143 \times 4 \times 7 =$$
$$143 \times 5 \times 7 =$$
$$143 \times 6 \times 7 =$$
$$143 \times 7 \times 7 =$$
$$143 \times 8 \times 7 =$$
$$143 \times 9 \times 7 =$$

4 Can you explain the patterns which emerge from the
following calculations?

(i)
$$(0 \times 9) + 1 =$$
$$(1 \times 9) + 2 =$$
$$(12 \times 9) + 3 =$$
$$(123 \times 9) + 4 =$$
$$(1234 \times 9) + 5 =$$
$$\vdots$$

(ii)
$$6 \times 7 =$$
$$66 \times 67 =$$
$$666 \times 667 =$$
$$6666 \times 6667 =$$
$$66666 \times 66667 =$$
$$\vdots$$

82 Surprising subtractions

Choose any four digits such as 3, 6, 2, 8 and rearrange them to form the largest and smallest numbers possible, namely 8632 and 2368.

Subtract the smaller number from the larger number and repeat the process using the four digits in the answer as the new starting point:

$$\begin{array}{r} 8632 \\ - 2368 \\ \hline 6264 \end{array} \qquad \begin{array}{r} 6642 \\ - 2466 \\ \hline 4176 \end{array} \qquad \begin{array}{r} 7641 \\ - 1467 \\ \hline 6174 \end{array}$$

In this example the digits 1, 4, 6, 7 occur in the answer at the second stage and no new numbers are generated from then on.

Investigate what happens with different sets of four digits as a starting point and continue subtracting until no new numbers occur. What do you notice?

What is the longest chain of subtractions you can find before nothing new occurs?

83 How large a number can you get?

Start with any six digits such as

$$5 \quad 3 \quad 9 \quad 7 \quad 2 \quad 4$$

and from them make two three-digit numbers, for example 324 and 579, where each digit has been used once only.

Now   (i) add your numbers   : $324 + 579 = \quad 903$
        (ii) multiply your numbers: $324 \times 579 = 187\,596$

The object is to find as large a sum and as large a product as you can.

Can you decide on a strategy which would always give you the largest answers first time? If you can you can challenge your friend to see who can first find the largest number from a given set of six digits.

Variations on this would be to make up three two-digit numbers and look for the largest sum and product, or start with seven digits say and consider a three-digit and four-digit number.

84 Four 4s

This well-tried activity has been responsible for many person-hours of interest and frustration. The idea is to express as many numbers as you can from 1 to 100 using exactly four 4s and any mathematical symbols you know.

For example

$$15 = \frac{44}{4} + 4 \quad \text{or} \quad (4 \times 4) - \frac{4}{4}$$

$$16 = (4 \times 4) + 4 - 4 \quad \text{or} \quad (4 \times \sqrt{4}) + (4 \times \sqrt{4})$$

There are often a number of ways of expressing the same number using four 4s as shown here but some numbers can be difficult to express. Apart from the four basic rules of $+$, $-$, $\times$, $\div$ and $\sqrt{}$ illustrated here you may find the following helpful.

4! means $4 \times 3 \times 2 \times 1 = 24$ and is called 'factorial four'

$$\frac{4}{\cdot 4} = 10$$

$\cdot\dot{4}$ means 0.4 recurring and is equal to $\frac{4}{9}$

$$\text{so} \quad \frac{4}{\cdot\dot{4}} = 9$$

You should now be able to find at least one way of expressing most, if not all, of the numbers from 1 to 100.

It may be fun to do this with a partner and challenge a pair of friends to see who can find the most in a given time.

85 What was the sum?

The result of dividing a two-digit number by a two-digit number with a calculator was as shown. What were the numbers?

$$0.4482758$$

86 Calculator words

Because of the way digits are formed on a calculator display they often look like letters when viewed upside down. Take, for example, the number 710.77345 which looks like this when displayed on a calculator.

Now view the display upside down and you should recognise a well-advertised petroleum product!

Because of this dual interpretation of the calculator display you can have a lot of interest and amusement.

Try 'translating' the following:

A calculator never tells 5317.

317537 went fishing off 3007 on a 0.717 for 3705 but only caught some 5733.

Instead of giving the numbers directly they can be replaced by calculations as the following passage illustrates.

$(68 \times 99) + 986$ decided to $(2486 + 3927 + 1322)$

$\sqrt{(264\,196)}$ walking $(10\,609 \times 5)$ because $(21\,386 \div 629)$

had a $(723 \times 48) + 303$ $(85^2 + 109)$ in one and a

$(2463 + 1977 - 736)$ in the other. They hurt like

$(85^2 + 20^2 + 10^2 + 3^2)$ and made him feel quite $(2 \times 5 \times 7 \times 11 + 1)$.

ShELL. OIL contains the additive Sh0ZZ.OIL. Remove it and what do you get?

Make a list of the digits on your calculator which, with a little imagination, can be interpreted as letters when viewed upside down. You will be surprised how many there are.

Next make a word list using these letters and their number equivalent. Do not forget that the order becomes reversed so that, for example, the word 'heel' is not represented by 4337 but by 7334.

Now you are in a position to write your own story incorporating 'calculator words'. Replace the words by their number equivalents or better, by calculations whose answer gives the number equivalent.

87 A calculator crossword

The clues are given below
in two forms, in word form and
number form.

Use one to check the other.

Word clue	Calculation
Across	*Across*
2. Far from the truth.	2. $\sqrt{(100\,489)}$
4. A large edible bird.	4. $185^2 + 781$
6. 4 across might have produced many precious ones.	6. 809×7
7. At the heart of campanology.	7. $10127 - 2389$
8. Bisect Isis.	8. $(72 \times 323) \div 456$
9. Part of the ear.	9. $2^2 + 5^2 + 23^2 + 57^2$
12. Boy's name.	12. $(467 \times 680) - 23$
14. Help! not quite.	14. $3789 \div 7578$

Down	*Down*
1. Cavities.	1. $[(188 \times 463) \div 23\cdot5] + 50\,000$
2. A heron often stands on one.	2. $7^2 \times 13$
3. A close friend of 12 across.	3. $11\,545 + 7265 + 12763$
5. Traders do this.	5. $85^2 + 22^2 + 5^2 + 1^2$
7. The Good Book.	7. 198×191
10. Busy workers.	10. $(57 + 16)^2 + 3^2$
11. Exists.	11. $2856 \div 56$
13. . . . and behold!	13. $(28 \times 18) \div 720$

When you have completed this crossword, try constructing your own.

88 A mining bonanza

In the outback of Australia a mining company made test drillings into a rich mineral reserve. The evidence of the survey was mapped out on a square grid and the value, in millions of pounds, of the deposits indicated by numbers as shown above.

Because of the lie of the land and the open-cast mining method employed the company must begin at the square marked 'Start' and move from square to square either up or down, or across. Diagonal moves are not possible, and the same square cannot be mined twice.

Find the most profitable route for the miners for the first thirteen squares they mine.

One route for example could follow the squares
24 70 6 77 30 66 22 73 19 98 1 90 14
This would give a profit of £590 million.
You can do better!

32	80	19	98	1	90	14	85
66	22	73	52	72	57	83	31
30	84	41	73	16	74	45	92
77	6	70	24	Start	28	67	11
32	99	44	81	27	75	42	98
68	21	72	56	59	42	75	17
34	87	19	92	5	99	27	88

89 Hundreds, tens and units

Take any three-digit number such as 235. Write down the number formed by putting its digits in reverse order, 532.

Subtract the smaller number from the larger.

$$\begin{array}{r} 532 \\ -\ 235 \\ \hline 297 \end{array}$$

Now write down the number formed by reversing the order of the digits in the answer and add to the answer.

$$\begin{array}{r} 297 \\ +\ 792 \\ \hline 1089 \end{array}$$

When you have tried this on a few more numbers you should be able to predict the answer and baffle your friends.

90 Magic circles

Put the numbers 1, 2, 3, 4, 5, 6 into the squares so that the numbers on each circle add up to the same amount. When this happens the circles are said to be magic.

Can you find an easy rule for giving six other numbers which could be put in the squares to make the circles magic?

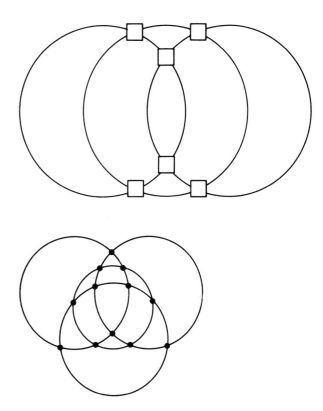

You should now be ready to tackle this magic circle puzzle for its solution is based on the same principle. Put one of the numbers 1, 2, 3, . . . , 10, 11, 12 at each intersection of the four circles in the diagram so that the circles are magic.

Is it obvious that the magic number for each circle is 39?

91 Prelude to a marathon

```
  F I T
+ M E N
-------
  J O G
```

Each letter stands for one of the digits 1, 2, 3, . . . 9. Each digit is used only once.

92 Find the digits

```
  A N T E
- E T N A
---------
  N E A T
```

There is a unique solution to this subtraction sum where each four-figure number has the same digits. Find it!

You might also like to find other examples of four letters which fit the same pattern and all form recognisable words.

93 Dr Numerati's telephone number

Dr Numerati was one of those people who are forever spotting relations between numbers. She noticed, for example, that the number of her house and those of two friends formed three consecutive prime numbers whose product was equal to her telephone number.

Dr Numerati lived between her friends and had a five-digit telephone number whose first digit was 6.

Find the number of Dr Numerati's house and of her telephone.

94 Make a century

By putting arithmetical signs in suitable places between the digits make the following sum correct:

$$1 \quad 2 \quad 3 \quad 4 \quad 5 \quad 6 \quad 7 \quad 8 \quad 9 \quad = \quad 100$$

There is more than one solution. See how many you can find.

95 Number wheels

The three numbers of each spoke and each edge of the wheel all add up to the same number. What is the number?

Find all the missing numbers.

Now arrange the numbers 1 to 19 in a similar wheel so that the total along each of the twelve lines is 22.

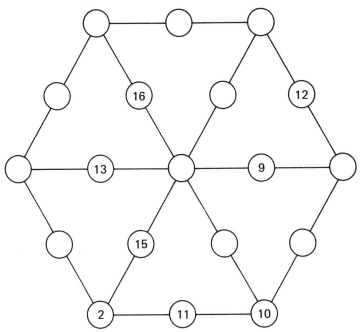

96 Some calculator challenges

(i) 56 406 is the product of two consecutive numbers. What are the two numbers?

(ii) 357 627 is the product of three consecutive odd numbers. Find them!

(iii) 1405 is the sum of two consecutive square numbers. What are they?

(iv) The volume of a cube is 200 cubic centimetres. Find the length of the edge of the cube as accurately as you can with your calculator.

97 Division patterns

1 Use your calculator to work out

$$\frac{1}{7} \quad \frac{2}{7} \quad \frac{3}{7} \quad \frac{4}{7} \quad \frac{5}{7} \quad \frac{6}{7}$$

as decimal fractions.

What do you notice about the first six digits which occur after the decimal place?

Without using your calculator, write down the decimal fractions for $\frac{8}{7}, \frac{9}{7}, \frac{16}{7}$, to 6 decimal places.

If the calculator you were using had a longer display what would the first twelve digits be for $\frac{1}{7}$? Can you see how to write down the recurring pattern for any division by 7?

With any division sum it is a fact that the division process terminates at some stage or it generates a sequence of recurring digits, for example

$$\frac{3}{16} = 0.1875$$

$$\frac{3}{7} = 0.428\,571\,428\,571\,428\,571 \ldots$$

When dividing by a number which can be expressed as a power of 2 multiplied by a power of 5 such as 16, 20, 64, 125, 320 then the division process will always terminate. Why? However, when dividing by any other number the division process will always lead to a sequence of recurring digits. With division by 7 you will have found a pattern of six digits recurring, and in general on division by a number n the recurring pattern will be of length $n-1$ or less. Can you explain this?

2 A calculator was used to investigate the patterns of digits when dividing by 17 but its capacity was not large enough to exhibit the full cycle of repeating digits. The following calculations gave

$$\frac{1}{17} = 0.058\,823\,5$$

$$\frac{2}{17} = 0.117\,647\,1 \qquad \frac{4}{17} = 0.235\,294\,1$$

$$\frac{3}{17} = 0.176\,470\,5 \qquad \frac{5}{17} = 0.294\,117\,6$$

Knowing that in this case the repeating pattern has sixteen digits write down what the sequence of recurring digits will be and give $\frac{5}{17}$ as a decimal fraction to twenty decimal places. Try to predict $\frac{6}{17}$, $\frac{7}{17}$, etc. before checking with your calculator.

3 Try finding the repeating pattern of digits when dividing by 19 using as few calculator divisions as possible.

4 Now try finding patterns for division by other numbers, 11 and 13 for example are particularly interesting.

98 Some named numbers

Palindromic numbers

These are numbers such as 25452 which read the same forwards as backwards.

Not counting single-digit numbers, which is the smallest palindromic prime and which the smallest palindromic square number?

How many other palindromic square numbers are there less than 1000?

There are five palindromic primes between 100 and 200; which are they? Why are there no palindromic primes between 400 and 700? Show that all the palindromic numbers between 1000 and 2000 have a factor in common.

Amicable pairs

Some pairs of numbers have the fascinating connection that the factor sum of each is equal to the other. This mutual support between two numbers has captured the imagination of some mathematicians who have named them *amicable pairs*.

The smallest such pair is 220 and 284.

$220 : 1 + 2 + 4 + 5 + 10 + 11 + 20 + 22 + 44 + 55 + 110 = 284$

$284 : 1 + 2 + 4 + 71 + 142 = 220$

Euler made a study of such pairs and in 1750 published a list of 60 of them. Surprisingly he missed the second smallest pair, 1184 and 1210, and these were not discovered until 1866 when a 16 year old boy Paganini found them.

Find the divisors of this pair and check their close interconnection.

Further pairs to investigate are

| 2620 | 6232 | 17 296 |
| 2924 | 6368 | 18 416 |

99 Magic stars

Put numbers in the empty circles of stars (a) and (b) so that
the numbers along each line of *both* stars have the same total.

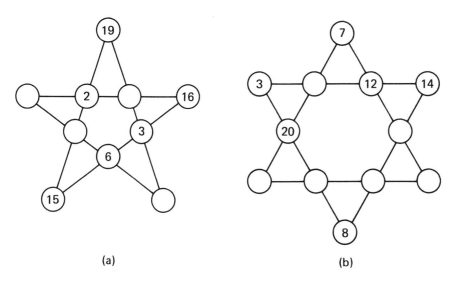

(a)   (b)

Stars (c) and (d) are also magic (i.e. the numbers along each
line have the same total) and each have the same magic
number. Further, the missing numbers in each case are 1, 3,
4, 5, and 7. What more help do you want!

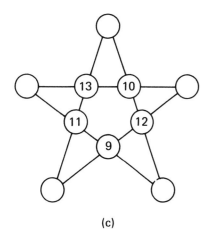   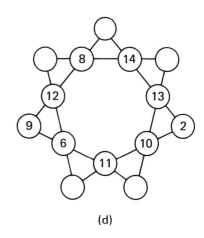

(c)   (d)

100 Safety first

(a) is an addition sum in disguise. Each letter stands for a
different digit. S, for example, represents 3. What do the
other letters represent?

(b) is another classic problem of the same kind.

```
    C R O S S
  +   R O A D S
    D A N G E R
```
(a)

```
    S E N D
  +   M O R E
    M O N E Y
```
(b)

56

101 The gambler's secret strategy

A gambler made three dice.
The red dice had the numbers 2, 4, 9 twice on its faces.
The blue dice had the numbers 3, 5, 7 twice on its faces.
The yellow dice had the numbers 1, 6, 8 twice on its faces.

The total on the faces of each dice was the same but the gambler was confident that if he let his opponent choose a dice first and roll it he could select a dice which would give him a better chance of obtaining a higher score. Explain!

102 The transportation problem

Three bus companies Aristotle, Bacchus and Copernicus provide the buses to transport the children home from the four schools, Piltdown, Queen's, Ruritania and Scholars.

To transport all the children the number of buses required at the schools are

$$P: 8 \quad Q: 5 \quad R: 7 \quad S: 5$$

and the bus companies have suitable buses at their depots as follows:

$$A: 9 \quad B: 6 \quad C: 10$$

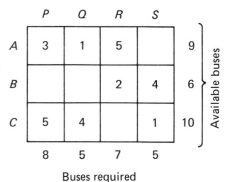

	P	Q	R	S	Available buses
A	3	1	5		9
B			2	4	6
C	5	4		1	10
Buses required	8	5	7	5	

	P	Q	R	S
A	3	2	5	1
B	2	1	3	4
C	5	6	4	8

The first table shows one of the many possible ways in which the bus companies could allocate their buses to the schools.

The next table shows the distance in miles from the bus depots to the schools, for example it shows that from C to Q is 6 miles.

Naturally the education authority wishes to keep its costs as low as possible so it wants to find the best way of allocating the buses from the depots to the schools so as to reduce the total mileage covered.

The above allocation gives a total bus mileage of

$$(3 \times 3) + (1 \times 2) + (5 \times 5) + (2 \times 3) + (4 \times 4) + (5 \times 5) + (4 \times 6) + (1 \times 8)$$

$$= \quad 9 \quad + \quad 2 \quad + \quad 25 \quad + \quad 6 \quad + \quad 16 \quad + \quad 25 \quad + \quad 24 \quad + \quad 8$$

$$= 115 \; miles$$

By making better use of the shorter routes the total mileage can be much reduced. In fact it can be made as low as 67 miles. How?

103 Further number patterns

1 $3^2 - 2^2 = 9 - 4 = 5 = 3 + 2$
   $4^2 - 3^2 = 16 - 9 = 7 = 4 + 3$
   $5^2 - 4^2 = 25 - 16 = 9 = 5 + 4$

Explain the pattern and show that it is always true.

2 $3^2 = 9$ $2 \times 4 = 8$
   $4^2 = 16$ $3 \times 5 = 15$
   $5^2 = 25$ $4 \times 6 = 24$

Extend the pattern. Is it true for large numbers?

3 Investigate the successive powers of a whole number
   such as 3 3^2 3^3 3^4 3^5 . . .

In particular note the pattern formed by the last digit.

4 Complete the following and continue for two more lines:

$$1 =$$
$$3 + 5 =$$
$$7 + 9 + 11 =$$
$$13 + 15 + 17 + 19 =$$

Can you make a general statement to describe the pattern?

5 Complete the following patterns and make an observation
   on what you find:

$$1 = \qquad\qquad\qquad 1^3 =$$
$$1 + 2 = \qquad\qquad 1^3 + 2^3 =$$
$$1 + 2 + 3 = \qquad\quad 1^3 + 2^3 + 3^3 =$$
$$1 + 2 + 3 + 4 = \qquad 1^3 + 2^3 + 3^3 + 4^3 =$$

104 Pythagorean triads

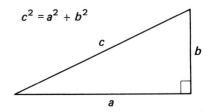

$$c^2 = a^2 + b^2$$

Pythagoras' theorem relating the lengths of the sides of a
right-angled triangle is well known. Also widely known is
the fact that a triangle whose sides are in the ratio 3 : 4 : 5
is right-angled as $3^2 + 4^2 = 5^2$.

The Pythagorean triads are sets of whole numbers like
3, 4 and 5 which satisfy the relation $a^2 + b^2 = c^2$ and can
thus be used as the lengths of sides for a right-angled triangle.

Use your calculator to produce a table of the squares of
the numbers from 1 to 50 and see how many triads you can
find.

Can you find two different right-angled triangles with
whole-number sides whose areas are equal?

A similar problem in three dimensions is to find possible lengths for the edges of a cuboid (i.e. a rectangular box) so that the edges and the diagonal are all whole numbers.

$$a^2 + b^2 + c^2 = d^2$$

One solution is

$$1^2 + 2^2 + 2^2 = 3^2$$

Can you find some more?

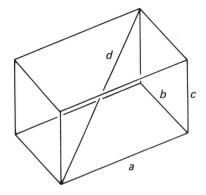

105 Intriguing multiplications

Playing with her calculator one day Rosemary multiplied together the numbers 159 and 48 and obtained 7632. On reflection she realised that the equation

$$159 \times 48 = 7632$$

contained each of the digits 1, 2, . . . , 9 once only. She could hardly believe her luck and felt the result must be unique. But she was wrong! There are several other pairs of numbers whose product gives a sum which uses all the digits only once. Can you find any of them?

Another intriguing product is

$$16\,583\,742 \times 9 \ = \ 149\,253\,678$$

where all the digits occur once on each side of the equality sign. Can you find any other products with this property?

106 A magic diamond

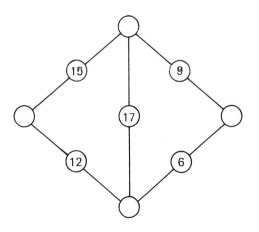

Find numbers to put in the circles so that the total along each line of the diamond is the same.

107 Palindromic dates

On 28 September 1982, a radio commentator
drew attention to the interesting pattern of
numbers in the date 28.9.82, when written in its
usual abbreviated form. This set young Susan
Nasus, the form swot, thinking about the
distribution of such palindromic dates. She soon
came to the conclusion that some years were
richer in such dates than others and set herself
the task of finding the two closest palindromic
dates in this century. What do you make them?

108 'Mind reading' number cards

Imagine you had a set of weights consisting of
one each of

1 kg   2 kg   4 kg   8 kg   16 kg

With these it would be possible to weigh
any whole number of kilograms from
1 kg to 31 kg.

Copy and complete the following table
up to 31 to show which weights are used.

	16	8	4	2	1
1					✓
2				✓	
3				✓	✓
4			✓		
5			✓		✓
6			✓	✓	
7			✓	✓	✓
8		✓			
9		✓			✓
10		✓		✓	
11		✓		✓	✓
12		✓	✓		
13		✓	✓		✓
14		✓	✓	✓	
15		✓	✓	✓	✓
16	✓				
17	✓				✓

```
┌─────────────────────────────┐
│  1     3     5     7         │
│                             │
│  9    11    13    15         │
│                             │
│  17   19    21    23         │
│                             │
│  25   27    29    31         │
└─────────────────────────────┘
```

Now cut out five squares of card say 10 cm × 10 cm and with a felt pen on the first card put clearly all the numbers which correspond to a mass which needed the 1 kg weight. The result is shown here in the diagram.

On the second card put all the numbers which correspond to a mass which needed the 2 kg weight (i.e. 2, 3, 6, 7, 10, 11, etc.); on the third card put all the numbers which correspond to a mass which needed the 4 kg weight in its weighing, and so on.

You should now have five cards each with sixteen numbers on them. To check that you have them right, turn to the back of this book.

The game is to ask a friend to think of a number from 1 to 31 and then show her each of your cards in turn. If her number is on a card she is to respond 'Yes', if not, 'No'. By the time she has finished saying 'Yes' or 'No' to the last card you should be able to tell her the number she had thought of! 'How?' you may well ask.

Suppose your friend thinks of 21, then this will be on three cards, the 1 kg card, the 4 kg card and the 16 kg card. All you do is add together 1 + 4 + 16, the cards to which your friend responded 'Yes' to, and you will have 21. To help it is useful to put a 1, 2, 4, 8 or 16 on the back of the appropriate card so that you can see it, but small enough so that your friend will probably not notice it. You can then shuffle the cards in any order and not look at the side you show your friend at all which will baffle her even more.

Try to practise the use of your cards with someone else in the family so you develop a slick technique before trying it on your friends.

You can start again and make a table up to 63 using one additional weight of 32 kg. Then you will need six cards with 32 numbers on each.

109 3 × 3 magic squares

A magic square is a square of numbers in which every row, column and diagonal add up to the same total such as the example in (a) where every line totals 24, its magic number.

Complete magic squares (b) and (c) by first finding their magic numbers from the completed line of numbers.

11	3	10
7	8	9
6	13	5

(a)

6		
7	5	3

(b)

		10
	7	
4		5

(c)

Now try (d) and (e), where more numbers are given to you but the reasoning is not so straightforward.

14	3	
		13
8	15	

(d)

11	1	
9		7
	15	5

(e)

The formation of magic squares is an ancient pastime and records of them go back in China to before Christ. The basic 3×3 square for example is attributed to the Chinese Emperor Yu who reigned around 2200 BC. Their fascination has not diminished with time as recent books on the subject testify.

All 3×3 magic squares have essentially one pattern which is that of the square formed from the numbers 1, 2, 3, . . . , 9 (see (f)).

Other magic squares could be formed from this by, for example, increasing all the numbers by a given number, say 6. Alternatively the numbers 1 to 9 could be replaced by the first nine odd numbers 1, 3, 5, . . . , 17.

There is another interesting way for generating a set of nine numbers which will form a 3×3 magic square which is not so obvious.

8	1	6
3	5	7
4	9	2

(f)

Take any number to start (e.g. 3), then decide on two different numbers (e.g. 2 and 5) which will be added to the original number as shown below.

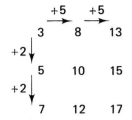

Now take these numbers in the order

3   8   13   5   10   15   7   12   17

and in this order replace the numbers 1 to 9 in the basic square. The result is magic square (g) with magic number 30.

Now produce some magic squares of your own.

Would this method work with decimal numbers or some negative numbers?

Can you prove it to be generally true?

12	3	15
13	10	7
5	17	8

(g)

110 4 × 4 and higher order magic squares

The first evidence of magic squares being investigated in Europe was in the early part of the fifteenth century. Agrippa constructed magic squares of all orders from 3 to 9 which he associated with the earth's planets then known. People through the ages have always held a mysticism for numbers (we still say 'third time lucky' and often believe 13 to be unlucky, for example) and magic squares have their own particular aura. The artist Dürer did a woodcut which he called *Melancholy* in which the date of its execution 1514 appears as part of a 4 × 4 magic square in the picture.

16	3	2	13
5	10	11	8
9	6	7	12
4	15	14	1

In this magic square the rows, columns and main diagonals all total 34. There are also many other sets of four symmetrically placed numbers in the square which total 34 such as

16   13   4   1   and   3   8   14   9

What other sets can you find?

With the numbers 1, 2 . . . , 16 it is possible to make 880 fundamentally different 4 × 4 magic squares. These were first all published in 1693 by Frénicle. Not all these possess all the symmetries of Dürer's square above. Some, classified as *simple*, possess only the basic requirement to be magic while others, classified as Nasik, are considered the most perfect and contain even more symmetry than Dürer's square. Here are examples of each.

7	6	11	10
14	9	8	3
12	15	2	5
1	4	13	16

Simple

1	14	7	12
15	4	9	6
10	5	16	3
8	11	2	13

Nasik

Find as many sets of four symmetrically placed numbers in each which total 34. Make yourself some square counters, number them 1 to 16 and see how many different 4×4 magic squares you can find.

There are no particularly neat ways of constructing magic squares of even order but with squares of odd order the following method due to Bachet de Méziriac is worth knowing. It is illustrated here for a 5×5 magic square but is equally applicable to any odd order.

3	16	9	22	15
20	8	21	14	2
7	25	13	1	19
24	12	5	18	6
11	4	17	10	23

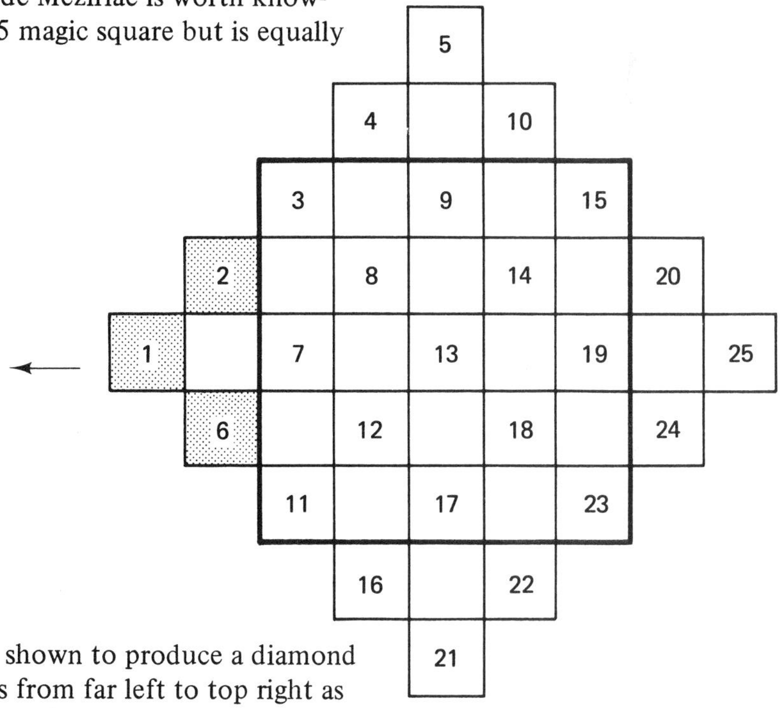

←

```
                5
          4        10
     3        9        15
 2        8        14        20
1     7       13       19        25
 6       12       18       24
    11       17       23
        16       22
            21
```

First border the 5×5 square as shown to produce a diamond shape. Now number the diagonals from far left to top right as shown. Next imagine sliding the numbers outside the original square into the spaces on the opposite side of the square without changing their arrangement. The result is a magic square.

One magic square which deserves a special mention is Euler's 8 × 8 solution which is also a knight's tour (see activity 44). It was obviously not known to H. E. Dudeney the famous Victorian puzzler who, writing about the possibility of such a magic square existing, says 'Can a perfect solution be found? I am convinced that it cannot, but it is only a pious opinion.'

111 A magic cube

27 unit cubes are numbered
from 1 to 27. There are several
ways in which they can be
made into a 3 x 3 x 3 cube so
that any row of unit cubes
parallel to an edge of the main
cube correspond to numbers
which total 42. The long
diagonals of the cube also
total 42 but not the diagonals
of the faces. The diagram
shows the arrangement for the
top layer for one solution. Can
you find the arrangements for
the other two layers?

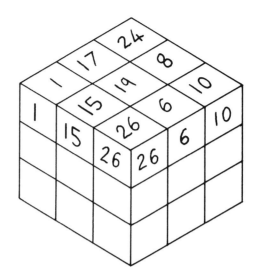

112 A question of balance

In a box there are 27 new red snooker balls all looking
exactly alike. However it is known that one of them is faulty
and weighs more than the others. Given that you have a
balance but no weights show how, by comparing sets of balls
against each other, you can find the faulty ball in only three
balances.

113 Further calculator challenges

(i)   What is the remainder on dividing 89 328 by 729?
(ii) Find a way of using the $\sqrt{}$ function to help in evaluating
      $\sqrt[3]{200}$.
(iii) What is the smallest number x which gives the answer 0
      to the calculation $1/x$ on your calculator?

114 A weighing problem

A greengrocer had a pair of scales and four weights. The weights were such that with them he could correctly weigh any whole number of kilograms from 1 to 40.

How heavy was each weight and how could he manage to weigh all the different weights?

115 Similar rectangles

A sheet of rectangular paper is such that when it is folded in half it forms a rectangle of exactly the same shape as the original. What can be said about the lengths of its sides?

116 Designing a new dartboard

There seems to be no mathematical logic in the distribution of the numbers around a traditional dartboard. One way of overcoming this would be to redesign a board to maximise the sum of the gaps between the numbers around the board. Investigate!

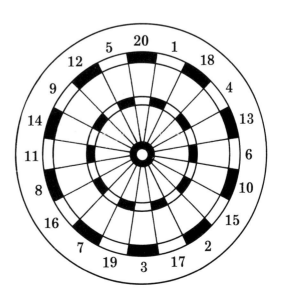

67

117 The only magic hexagon

Fill in the hexagons with the numbers 1, 2, 3, . . . , 19 so that the total of the numbers on every vertical path and on every diagonal path is always the same.

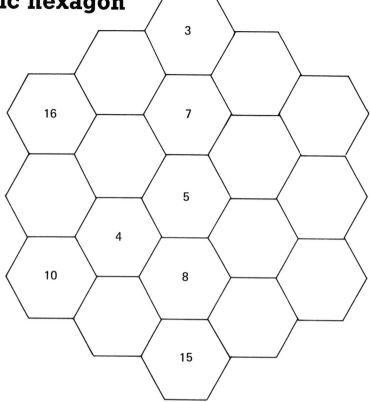

118 Nim

The game of Nim is for two people and appears to be simplicity itself. You need a supply of counters (matchsticks or drawing pins would do) and the game starts with the counters arranged arbitrarily in a number of heaps. In the example shown here there are three heaps with 7, 9 and 6 counters.

Each player in turn can remove as many counters as he likes from one of the heaps (he can if he wishes remove all the counters in a heap, but he must take at least one). The winner is the player who removes the last counter.

There is much more to this game than might first appear. See if you can develop some winning strategy.

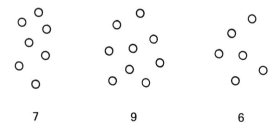

7   9   6

119 Triangulating a square

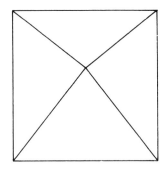

The square shown has been divided up into four triangles. All but one of these triangles is acute angled. Is it possible to divide a square into triangles so that all the triangles are acute angled? You may use as many triangles as you think necessary.

120 Who is 'it'?

In a children's game the person to be 'it' was decided by the children standing in a circle and chanting a counting rhyme which had 13 words. The count went clockwise around the circle, successively eliminating every 13th child. There were eight children $a, b, \ldots, h$ and the last child left in was c. Where did the count start?

121 Find the cards on the table

A number of playing cards of one suit were arranged in a circle on the table in such a way that the total of the face values of any set of three adjacent cards differed by at most one from the total for any similar set. The highest and lowest cards on the table were the 10 and 2 of diamonds. The 6 of diamonds was also in the circle.

Which cards were on the table and what was their order?

122 Dividing the inheritance

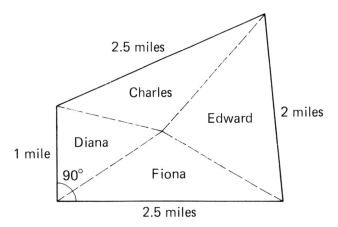

When a sheep farmer in Australia died, he left a will leaving
all his land to his four children, Charles, Diana, Edward and
Fiona. To avoid any squabbling over the land he made a
sketch on the ranch, which was in the shape of a quadrilateral
and decreed that the land be divided into four triangular
portions of equal area as indicated.

The initial reaction of the children was very favourable.
It was only when they tried to put his plan into action that
they realised they had a problem.

What was it?

123 The end of the world!

A group of religious fanatics decided, after intensive study
of their holy books and endless use of a powerful modern
computer, that the end of the world would occur when the
first day of a century next fell on a Sunday.

How much longer do they give us?

124 The sponsored marathon

Instead of asking her sponsors for a fixed sum of money,
say 3p, for each mile completed in the marathon (26 miles),
a runner struck on a clever idea to boost the proceeds for
her chosen charity. She persuaded her sponsors that as each
mile was progressively harder to run she would be happy if
they gave her only 1p for the first mile, 2p for the second
mile, 4p for the third mile and so on, doubling their sponsor-
ship for each additional mile completed.

The argument sounded plausible but when the runner
completed the marathon and called on her sponsors they
were in for a nasty shock. What was it?

125 The effect of inflation

The house which was first sold for £3500 when new in 1961
was sold in 1981 at a price of £34 000. The house has
remained essentially unchanged in this period. What annual
rate of inflation is this equivalent to assuming that the rate
remained unchanged?

In 1965 petrol cost 33p a gallon whilst in the summer of
1983 its price had risen to 184p a gallon. Does this represent
a higher or a lower rate of inflation than that of the house
price?

Assuming the same rates of inflation until the end of the
century, what will be the price of the house and of a gallon
of petrol in the year 2000?

126 Octogenarian occupations

A retired octogenarian mathematics teacher playing around
with a calculator given to him by his young teenage great
granddaughter discovered that the difference between the
cubes of the digits of his own age equalled the square of his
great granddaughter's age. How old were they?

127 Tails up!

The three coin puzzles here are of a kind, but are not all
possible. Which is the odd one out?

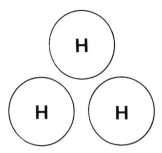

1 Place three coins on the table with heads uppermost. A
move consists of turning any two coins over. How many
moves do you need to arrange for all the tails to be
uppermost?

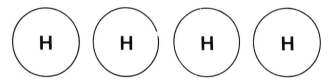

2 Place four coins on the table with heads uppermost. A
move consists of turning any three coins over. How many
moves do you need to arrange for all the tails to be
uppermost?

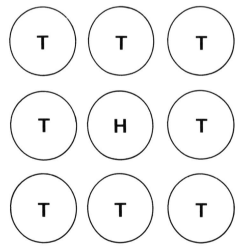

3 Place nine coins in a square array as shown with tails
uppermost apart from the coin in the centre. A move
consists of turning over the three coins in any row, or
any column, or either of the two diagonals. How many
moves do you need to arrange for all the tails to be
uppermost?

128 Dovetailed

A master carpenter had been teaching his apprentices the art of making dovetail joints. After they had done several routine exercises to perfect their skills, he showed them a cube made from two pieces of wood which appeared to have dovetail joints in each of its four vertical faces. The vertical faces all looked identical, see the diagram. The carpenter challenged his apprentices to copy his cube but they were all baffled. It can be made, but how?

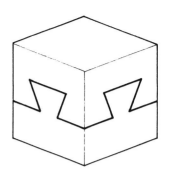

129 More matchstick mindbenders

Turn the spiral into three squares by moving four matches.

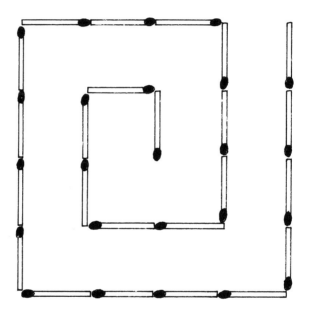

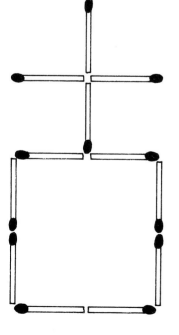

Convert this 'church with tower' symbol into three identical squares by moving five matches.

130 Bridging the river

In an initiative test two teams of Sandhurst cadets were challenged to build a 'bridge' across a river 5 metres wide. They had an unlimited supply of identical sleepers 4 metres long and could proceed *only* by piling one sleeper upon another.

How far from the bank is it possible for such a structure to reach with only three sleepers?

What is the smallest number of sleepers required to achieve the cadets' objective?

COMMENTARY

1 Matchstick triangles

The secret here is to think three-dimensionally and form a tetrahedron.

2 A tricky river crossing

The showman must first take the goat across. He then takes the wolf across and brings the goat back. He next takes the cabbage across and finally returns to collect the goat.

3 The baffled engine driver

This puzzle can seem quite impossible until you find the solution. It has much in common with puzzle 18. The key is to shunt C onto the main line by itself as shown below.

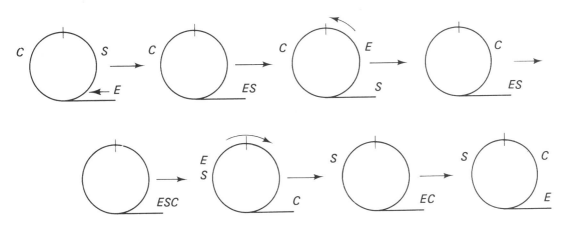

4 Make your own dice

If you could do this correctly without a model you have a good spatial sense.

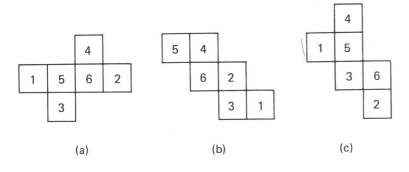

(a)   (b)   (c)

5 Map folding

Number the map on both sides then fold as shown below.

Then partly open out and pinching together 5 and 4 fold them so that 5 comes next to 6. 4 will then be next to 3 and it is an easy matter to pinch 1 and 2 together and fold them so that 1 is on top of 2 and 2 on top of 3.

6 The ingenious milkman

First fill the 3 pt jug. Next pour the 3 pints from this jug into the 5 pt jug. Again fill the 3 pt jug and then pour from it into the partially filled 5 pt jug until it is full. This leaves exactly 1 pint in the 3 pt jug.

It would thus be possible to measure any whole number of pints by measuring single pints in this way. Clearly there are more efficient ways for measuring most quantities. 5 pints and 3 pints can be measured directly and as 6 = 3 + 3 while 8 = 5 + 3, 6 pints and 8 pints are easily measured. But what about 7 pints and 4 pints?

7 Pawns on a chessboard

The solution shown here for this classical chessboard problem is a special case of the fact that it is possible to place $2n$ counters on an $n \times n$ board so that no three counters are in line

Note the line of symmetry which is often a feature in the solution of this type of problem.

8 Avoid three

This game is closely related to the previous puzzle but is complementary to it. Here, a player's strategy is to look for positions of the pieces which limit his opponent's play and force him into making a move with three in a line.

9 Two halves make a whole

This is an easy puzzle of its kind. The two pieces are each equivalent to a square and half a square as shown. It is surprising how many shapes can be made from them. To achieve all the shapes shown one of the pieces will need to be turned over. Which of the shapes can be made without doing this?

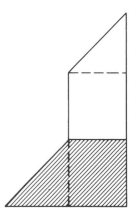

10 Cubism

A and *D* are the same.

11 Matchstick squares

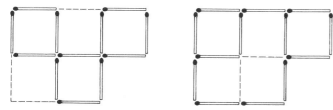

12 Curves of pursuit

Approximating to a curved path as a sequence of small steps is of fundamental importance in mathematics and is at the heart of calculus and numerical methods. The result not only makes an attractive drawing but can also be produced using coloured thread or wool (i) stitched through a piece of card or (ii) stretched between panel pins (i.e. small nails) hammered into a piece of plywood. In these activities a new line cannot be drawn until the previous one has been completed. They should not be confused with the more familiar ones where an equal number of points is marked off on two lines (or curves) to start with and then the points joined by lines as shown in the two examples on the next page.

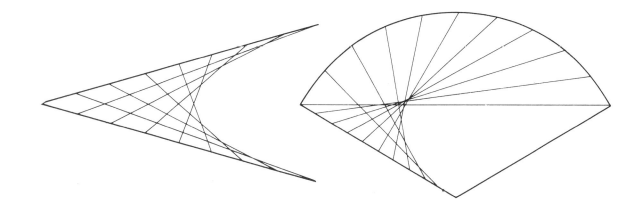

15 The army's predicament

This puzzle has much in common with puzzle 2 and
puzzle 20 and has been in circulation in some form since
the early part of this century. The solution here depends on
the fact that the canoe can hold two boys but it only needs
one boy to take the canoe across the river. One boy paddles
the canoe to the soldiers on the left bank. A soldier then
paddles himself and his kit to the right bank where he stays.
The second boy now paddles the boat to the left bank,
collects the first boy and returns to the right bank. This
process is repeated until each soldier has crossed the river.

16 The farmer's sheep-pens

Triangular sheep pens may be unorthodox
but it solves the problem.

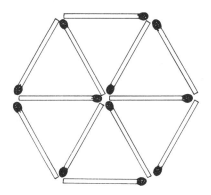

17 The knight's dance

Sixteen moves are required. They are best thought of as four groups of moves in which the four knights move from corner squares to middle squares, and vice versa in a kind of square dance in which they rotate as a foursome about the centre square. This puzzle has been known for a long time. The first record of it in Europe dates back to 1512.

 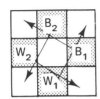 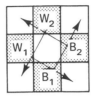

18 The railway sidings

This is another shunting puzzle which became popular in the early part of this century. Like most of its kind it is tantalising because it is easy to state but until it has been solved the puzzler may well think it is unsolvable. It often helps to use some coloured bricks (or matchboxes) to represent the trucks and the engine.

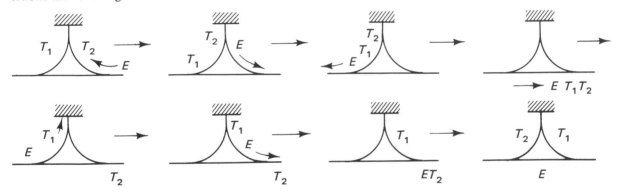

19 The multi-coloured cube

Paint each one centimetre cube in such a way that the three faces meeting at one corner are all red and the three faces meeting at the opposite corner are all blue. The eight cubes can then be fitted together to make either a red two-centimetre cube or a blue two-centimetre cube.

The three-centimetre cube is a much harder problem and it might require a visual aid – try colouring sugar lumps. The colouring is possible. The 27 one-centimetre cubes have 27×6 square faces while the three three-centimetre cubes have 3×6 faces each made of nine squares. Thus there are just the right number of squares to go round if they can be correctly coloured.

In a red three-centimetre cube the smaller cubes appear in four distinct ways.

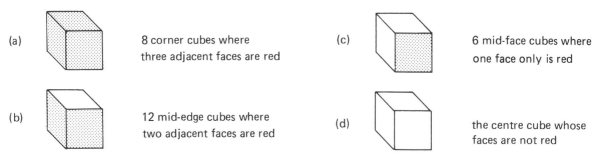

(a) 8 corner cubes where three adjacent faces are red

(b) 12 mid-edge cubes where two adjacent faces are red

(c) 6 mid-face cubes where one face only is red

(d) the centre cube whose faces are not red

There must be the same numbers of blue cubes and yellow cubes for a solution to exist and considerations like this lead to the following solution:

6 cubes coloured $R_2B_2Y_2$
3 cubes coloured $R_3B_2Y_1$ The letter indicates the colour
3 cubes coloured $R_3B_1Y_2$ and the suffix the number of
3 cubes coloured $R_2B_3Y_1$ faces of that colour. Where
3 cubes coloured $R_2B_3Y_1$ there are two or three faces
3 cubes coloured $R_1B_3Y_2$ of the same colour they are
3 cubes coloured $R_2B_1Y_3$ always next to each other.
3 cubes coloured $R_1B_2Y_3$
1 cube each
coloured R_3B_3 B_3Y_3 Y_3R_3

The notation has been invented for the problem and is very helpful in describing the different cubes. This is a typical device used by mathematicians who will use letters and symbols to suit the problem in hand rather than many words.

20 The jealous husbands

As with the previous puzzle it is helpful to develop some kind of notation to describe the situation. Here the couples are denoted by Aa, Bb, Cc etc., where the capital letter stands for the husband and the small letter for his wife.

With three couples the boat will need to be rowed across the water five times. One solution is given below:

	abc →	a ←	ABC →	A ←	Aa →
Aa	$A \mid a$	$Aa \mid$	$a \mid A$	$Aa \mid$	$\mid Aa$
Bb	$B \mid b$	$B \mid b$	$\mid Bb$	$\mid Bb$	$\mid Bb$
Cc	$C \mid c$	$C \mid c$	$\mid Cc$	$\mid Cc$	$\mid Cc$
	1	2	3	4	5

First the three wives *abc* row across and then wife *a* rows the boat back. Next the three husbands *ABC* row to safety leaving wife *a* at the hotel and finally husband *A* returns to rescue his courageous wife!

You may find this puzzle easier to solve by using labelled pieces of paper to represent the people.

The following solution with five couples satisfies all the conditions but it takes eleven crossings and you may find a better one. If you do the author would like to hear from you.

$\xrightarrow{abc}$ $\xleftarrow{a}$ $\xleftarrow{}$	$\xrightarrow{ad}$ $\xleftarrow{a}$ $\xleftarrow{}$	$\xrightarrow{BCD}$	$\xleftarrow{Dd}$ $\xrightarrow{ADE}$	$\xleftarrow{D}$ $\xrightarrow{Dd}$	$\xleftarrow{b}$ $\xrightarrow{abe}$
Aa	Aa	Aa	Aa	a | A	a | A	Aa
Bb	B | b	B | b	Bb	Bb	Bb	Bb
Cc	C | c	C | c	Cc	Cc	Cc	Cc
Dd	Dd	D | d	Dd	d | D	Dd	Dd
Ee	Ee	Ee	Ee	e | E	e | E	Ee

First the three wives *abc* row across and wife *a* returns with the boat. Then wives *a* and *d* row across, wife *d* gets out and *a* returns the boat. Now *BCD* row across and *Dd* row back leaving couples *Bb* and *Cc* in safety. The three husbands *ADE* now row across leaving their three wives *ade* temporarily at the hotel. *D* returns to pick up his wife. (NB *D* does not get out of the boat or he would be on the bank with *a* and *e* when their husbands were not present.) Finally *b* returns to fetch *a* and *e*.

21 The extension lead

This is a new version of another traditional puzzle. If you imagine the room rather like a shoe box and you open it up to form its net then the shortest distance from *A* to *B* is a route across the floor, a side wall and the ceiling whose length is 40 ft.

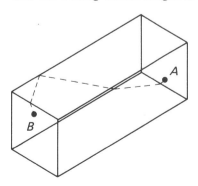

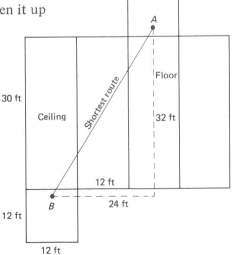

23 The square, cross and circle

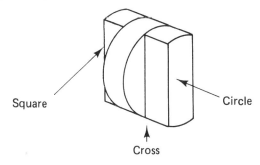

Square

Circle

Cross

24 The Möbius band

The results here are always very surprising to the person
meeting them for the first time. With a systematic approach
it should be possible to find a pattern relating the number of
twists in a band and the subsequent result of cutting down
the middle. At one level this activity is enormous fun but it
also has a serious side in posing questions about the nature of
different surfaces. See for example *Mathematics and the
Imagination* by E. Kasner and J. Newman (Bell), or
Experiments in Topology by S. Barr (John Murray).

25 The economical gardener

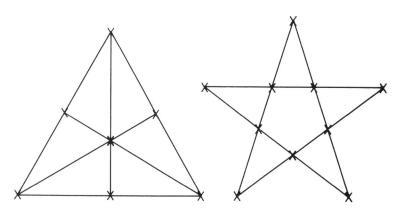

26 How many triangles can you see?

It will probably help to label all the points where lines intersect with letters and then label the triangles using the letters. Although this puzzle may appear to have much in common with the previous one it requires a different approach. First record, for example, all the triangles which have *AB* as a side, then *AC* etc.

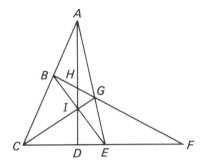

ABE	ABG	ABH	ABI
ACD	ACE	ACG	ACI
ADE	AEI	AGH	AGI
BCE	BCF	BCG	BCI
BEF	BEG	BGI	BHI
CDI	CEG	CEI	CFG
DEI	DFH	EFG	EGI
GHI			

By keeping the letters in alphabetic order it is easy to spot whether you have counted a triangle twice.

27 The unfriendly power-boats

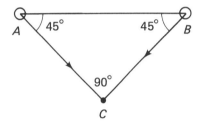

This is an interesting puzzle and might at first seem impossible.

No matter what path the boats follow they will not come together until the controller steers the boat to the point *C* shown in the above diagram. At this point the distance *AC* is equal to the distance *BC* and the bearing of *C* from *B* is 90° more than the bearing of *C* from *A*. When the boat from *A* reaches *C* by whatever path the boat from *B* will be there also.

28 The knight-guards

One solution of the knight's problem is shown here. Check yourself to see how each square is attacked.

There are analogous problems with the other chess pieces. For example, it can be achieved with five queens or nine kings or eight bishops. Have a go!

29 Reversing the trains

To handle this puzzle efficiently it is again necessary to develop some means of recording the moves made. It is also helpful to mark out the railway network on a larger scale and use some numbered counters to represent the trains. The following solution takes fifteen moves which are indicated by the arrows.

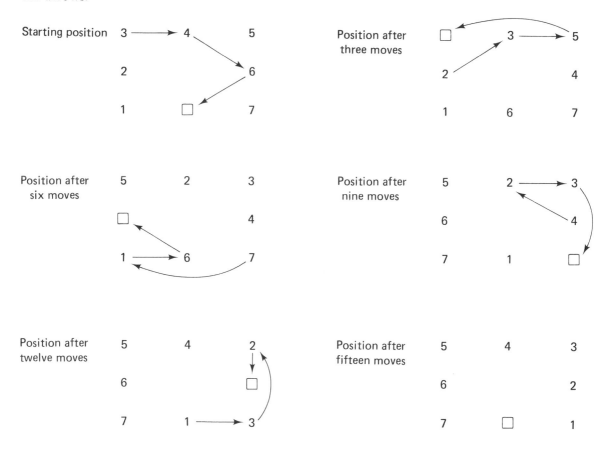

30 Quadruplets

Not only are the four pieces identical to each other, but they are the same shape as the original.

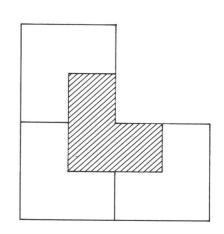

31 Complete the square

This puzzle is now available commercially in a variety of packs made of plastic pieces but you could easily make your own from coloured card.

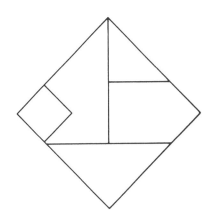

32 Roll a penny

A makes two revolutions. The queen's head will be upside down when penny *A* has rolled to the top of penny *B*, the correct way up when *A* is to the right of *B*, upside down when *A* is below *B* and the correct way when *A* is back at the start.

33 The growing network

This game must end in a limited number of moves because it starts with nine available arms (three points each with three arms) and each move uses up two arms and introduces a new point with one available arm. The effect of a move is thus to reduce the total number of available arms by one. There can thus be at most eight moves. There may be a fewer number of moves if one arm becomes isolated by the rest of the network.

These networks correspond to the different ways in which chemical atoms with a valency of 3 can join to make complex molecules.

34 Traversibility

$$A \to C \to E \to B \to D \to A \to B \to C \to D \to E \to A$$

There are many other possible solutions such as

$$A \to B \to C \to D \to A \to C \to E \to B \to D \to E \to A$$

A network is traversible if it can be drawn without taking the pencil off the paper or having to go over any line twice. The first network here is thus said to be traversible but the second one can only be drawn in four parts so the pencil has to be taken off the paper three times.

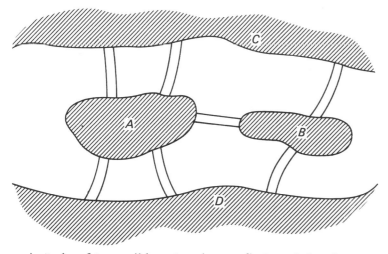

A study of traversible networks was first made by the mathematician Euler in the early part of the eighteenth century when he studied the now famous problem of the Königsberg bridges. Königsberg was a German town built on two islands and the banks of the River Pregel. The islands and river banks were connected by seven bridges as shown and the citizens of the town had, for many years, tried to find a way of starting from one point in the town, crossing every bridge once and then returning to their starting point. They could not find a way and when Euler became aware of the problem he was able to prove conclusively that the problem was incapable of solution. He first replaced the above map by a network which retained the significant features of the map where each region of the town was reduced to a point and the bridges by arcs. The problem now reduces to showing that this network cannot be drawn without taking your pencil from the paper.

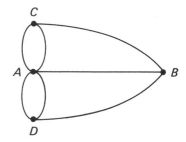

Euler realised that the key to the problem lay in the fact that the number of arcs meeting at A, B, C and D was odd – 3 at B, C and D, and 5 at A.

He showed that a point of a network with an odd number of arcs meeting at it (an odd node) could only be a starting point or a finishing point to trace the network, so the Königsberg problem which has 4 odd nodes cannot be solved.

To see why an odd node cannot be an intermediate point in a traversible network consider the 3-node P shown here with branches labelled 1, 2 and 3. In tracing a network in which P occurs let the first time the pencil comes to P be along 1. It can then leave via 2 say and at some stage it must return along 3, but then there is no route left to leave P which has not already been traced. Similar arguments can be used for any odd node and it follows that an odd node can only be used as a starting point or a finishing point. From this it can be shown that a network is only traversible if (i) all

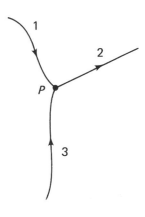

its nodes are even (i.e. have an even number of arcs meeting at them) or (ii) all its nodes are even except two which are odd and then they must be the starting point and the finishing point. The town of Königsberg could thus solve its problem by blowing up bridge *AB* for example or adding a second bridge from *A* to *B*. A good reference on this and related problems is *Mathematical Recreations and Essays* by W. W. Rouse Ball.

35 Impossible rotations!

Rotate the book about an edge through 180°, then about a line at 45° to this to obtain a 90° rotation as shown.

In general, a rotation of 180° about one axis followed by a rotation of 180° about an axis at an angle *x* to it is equivalent to a rotation through an angle 2*x* about an axis perpendicular to the original two axes.

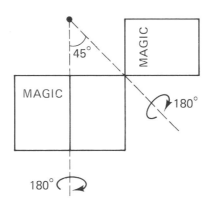

36 The hunter

A polar bear!

One solution starts at the north pole, see (a), but there are infinitely many possibilities near the south pole. For example, the hunter could start anywhere 3 miles north of the line of latitude which is 3 miles in circumference, see (b), . . . or 3 miles north of the line of latitude which is $1\frac{1}{2}$ miles in circumference . . . or etc.

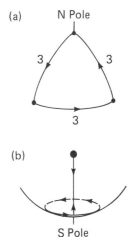

37 Four points in a plane

It is surprising that there are six arrangements in all, and you may well have given up before turning to the solutions shown here.

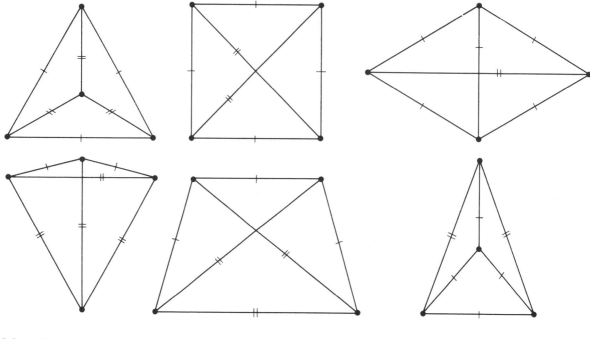

38 The letter dice

There must be a letter S opposite H. The arrangement of letters is shown in the net for the cube where it can be seen that there are in fact two letters S.

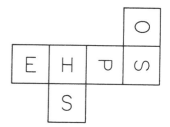

39 The queen's defence

The only two other fundamentally different solutions for the 4 × 4 board are shown here.

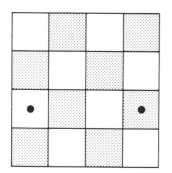 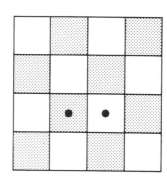

4 × 4 solutions

For a 5 x 5 board there are many solutions each requiring three queens. There are two more shown below. How many distinct solutions did you find?

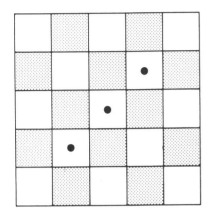 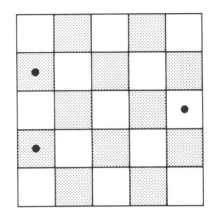

The 6 x 6 board can be solved with three queens too but in essentially only one way, while the 7 x 7 board requires four queens for its solution.

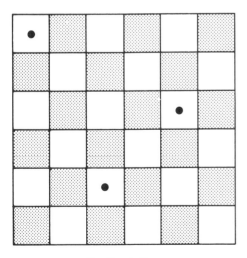

6 x 6 solution

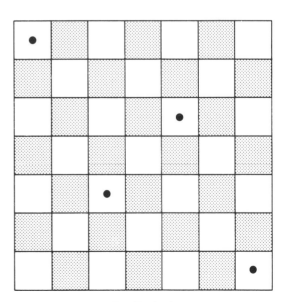

7 x 7 solution

With an 8 x 8 board the solution requires five queens and the solution given here also satisfies Jaenisch's further condition that no queen shall be under attack by another.

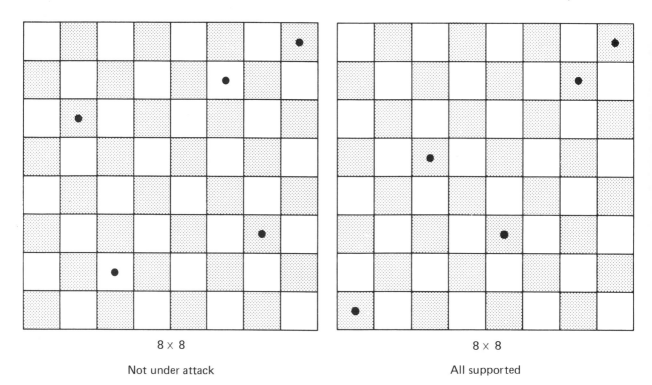

8 x 8

Not under attack

8 x 8

All supported

A good reference for further details on associated puzzles is *Mathematical Recreations and Essays* by W. W. Rouse Ball (Macmillan).

40 Seeing is believing

This is an old chestnut! The catch is that what looks like a diagonal of the 13 x 5 rectangle is in fact a very thin parallelogram whose area is 1 square unit.

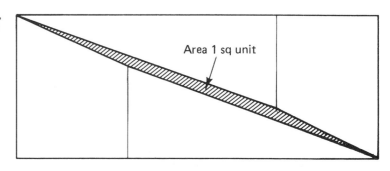

Area 1 sq unit

41 Inspecting the roads

A, C, E, G, H and I are odd nodes and because of this one of the roads to each of them will have to be driven over twice. To minimise the total distance to be covered the roads to be driven over twice can be arranged to be AG, HC and IE. One possible route is as follows:

$$A \to B \to C \to D \to E \to F \to A \to G \to F \to I \to E \to I \to D \to H \to C \to H \to B \to G \to H \to I \to G \to A$$

with a total distance of $(6 \times 13) + (9 \times 12) + (6 \times 5) = 216$ miles

42 Dominoes on a chessboard

It is impossible!

Imagine the domino painted half black and half white to match the chessboard squares. When two opposite squares of the board are removed the board loses two squares of the same colour. In the diagram given it is left with 30 black and 32 white squares so there is no way in which the dominoes can be placed to cover the board as each addition adds one black and one white square.

44 Knight's tours

A knight's tour is impossible on a 4 × 4 board but it is possible to find a path which visits fifteen squares. The 5 × 5, 6 × 6 and 7 × 7 tours are all possible, and a solution for each is shown here.

6	9	2	15
1	12	5	8
10	7	14	3
13	4	11	

4 × 4 no solution

1	14	9	20	3
24	19	2	15	10
13	8	25	4	21
18	23	6	11	16
7	12	17	22	5

5 × 5 solution

11	22	33	44	13	24	3
32	43	12	23	2	45	14
21	10	39	34	37	4	25
42	31	36	1	40	15	46
9	20	41	38	35	26	5
30	49	18	7	28	47	16
19	8	29	48	17	6	27

7 × 7 solution

1	32	9	22	7	30
10	23	36	31	16	21
33	2	17	8	29	6
24	11	26	35	20	15
3	34	13	18	5	28
12	25	4	27	14	19

6 × 6 solution

91

You may find, like the author and many people before him, that finding knight's tours becomes a fascination which you can return to on and off over a lifetime!

Small rectangles on which a knight's tour is possible are a 5 × 4 and 4 × 3.

1	20	7	16	3
6	15	2	11	8
19	10	13	4	17
14	5	18	9	12

5 × 4 solution

1	4	7	10
8	11	2	5
3	6	9	12

4 × 3 solution

The solutions to the crosses are shown below with the second solution a re-entrant path.

		2	15		
		13	10		
12	1	16	3	14	9
17	6	11	8	19	4
		18	5		
		7	20		

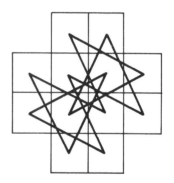

The solution of the 6 × 6 board shown above is a re-entrant path, due to the eighteenth century mathematician Euler, as the last square visited (36) is a knight's move from the first (1).

The reason a re-entrant path is not possible on a board with an odd number of squares depends on the fact that a knight's move always takes a knight to a square of a different colour. Suppose a tour starts on a black square then after an even number of moves it will have visited an odd number of squares and again be on a black square. This square, being the same colour as the starting square cannot be a knight's move from it.

A very good reference on this topic is *Mathematical Recreations and Essays*, by W. W. Rouse Ball (Macmillan).

45 Sawing up a cube

No matter how you try cutting up this cube there is no way
of getting away from the fact that the one-centimetre cube in
the centre has six faces all needing to be sawn, so the 27 cubes
cannot be achieved with fewer than six saw cuts.

46 The improbable hole

To show that it is possible to make a hole in a cube large
enough to pass a larger cube through it, it is necessary to
show that a cube has a cross-section larger than its square
face. Consider the rectangle $ABCD$ shown in the diagram.
A, B, C and D are each the same small distance from the
corner of the cube to which they are nearest. AB is clearly
longer than the edge PQ as it is at an angle to it. BC will be
longer than an edge as it is almost equal to the diagonal QR.
It would thus be possible to imagine a square hole cut through
the cube of a larger size than the face of the original cube.

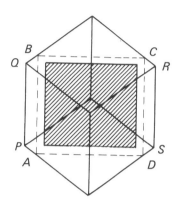

47 Identical twins

This is easy when you know how!

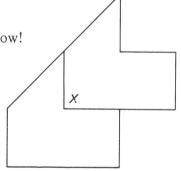

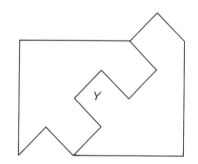

48 The four-colour theorem

Experience shows that people enjoy the challenge of trying
to find a map which cannot be coloured in fewer than five
colours and often think they have succeeded until someone
else shows how to re-colour it with four colours. The diagram
here shows how the given map can be coloured using only
four colours.

   Interestingly on the surface of a torus (like a beach ring)
it is possible to draw a map which cannot be coloured in less
than seven colours. See, for example, *What is Mathematics?* by
R. Courant and H. Robbins (Oxford University Press), or
Riddles in Mathematics by E. P. Northrop (Pelican).

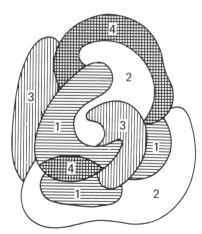

49 Mystifying match sticks

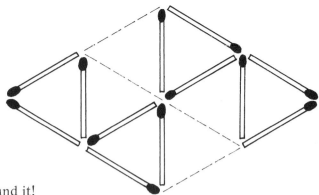

A very satisfying solution when you have found it!

50 Equilateral triangle to square

A neat way of seeing how to rearrange the pieces to form
the square is to imagine them hinged at *P*, *Q* and *R* and
rotating them into the square as shown here.

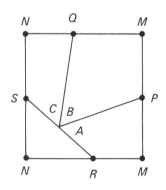

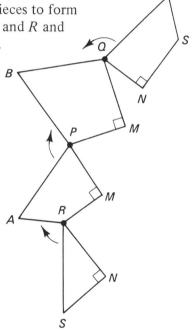

51 Squaring the urn

The key to this puzzle is in the pattern of circles from which
the urn is composed.

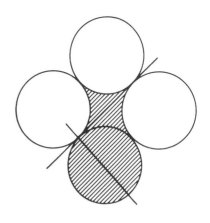

52 The baffled housewife

The apparent paradox is explained when Mrs Smith was
shown a timetable which showed the times of the P buses and
Q buses at her bus-stop.

P route	Q route
10.09	10.10
10.19	10.20
10.29	10.30
10.39	10.40
10.49	10.50
10.59	11.00

There is a gap of only one minute after a P bus visits the
stop until a Q bus is due, but then a gap of nine minutes
before the next P bus. Thus in any ten-minute period nine
minutes could be spent waiting for a P bus but only one
minute for a Q bus. The effect of this to a person using the
bus stop frequently would be to find that in nine times out
of ten a P bus would be the first to appear.

53 Invert the triangle

Three pennies need to be moved. Move the three corner
pennies as shown.

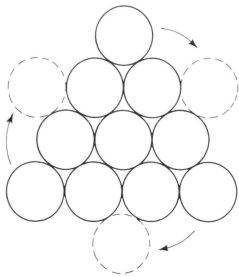

54 Avoid that snooker

In reality skilled players can impart spin to a ball which can significantly change the way in which it bounces off a side cushion. Nevertheless the method described in this activity gives a good idea of the appropriate direction to hit the cue ball to get out of a snooker.

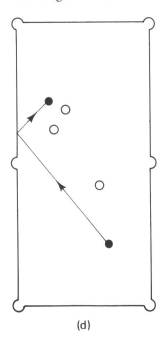

(d)

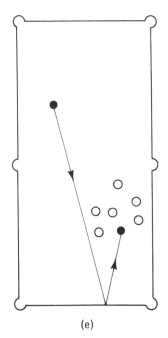

(e)

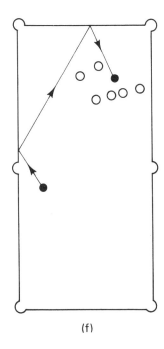

(f)

55 Squares

You need to be aware of squares at an angle as well as those the same way as the board. See those in the diagram here for example.

	X		O		
				X	
O					
X					O
			X		
		O			

56 The hungry bookworm

The answer is not 15 cm! The diagram here represents the view from the top of the books and the dotted lines show the bookworm's path which is only 9 cm long!

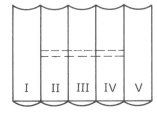

I II III IV V

57 Place the motorway junction

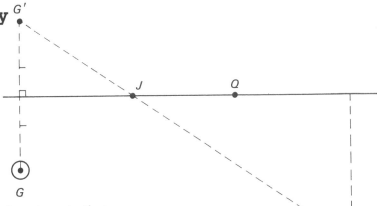

To solve this puzzle imagine the motorway as the line of a mirror and draw in the image of Green Glades. Now join this image to Pleasant Pastures by a straight line and the point where it crosses the motorway is the position for J.

To see why this gives the shortest route note that

$$GJ + JP = G'J + JP = G'J$$

If Q is any other point on the motorway then

$$GQ + QP = G'Q + QP > G'P$$

as $G'QP$ is a triangle and two sides together must always be longer than the third side.

58 Space filling

The larger tetrahedron cannot be made from smaller ones. When you remove a tetrahedron from each corner of the large tetrahedron the shape left in the centre is an octahedron with a square cross-section which cannot be made up of the smaller tetrahedra.

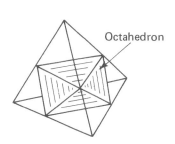

Octahedron

59 Curves from intersecting circles

If you want to practice using your compass then you should find this a satisfying exercise. Start by drawing a line across the middle of your page and mark off $\frac{1}{2}$ cm intervals to help in getting the correct radius for the circles. The technique for using a compass efficiently is (i) make sure the arms are tight at the joint, (ii) arrange the pencil or ball point pen so that its tip meets the compass point when the arms are together, (iii) concentrate on applying pressure at the point of the compass, (iv) do not try moving the compass by holding the pencil.

Perhaps the most obvious family of curves other than ellipses is that of the hyperbolae.

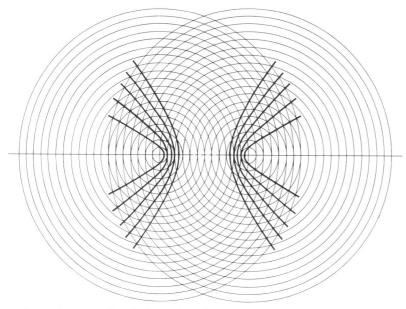

A good source book for other drawings of this kind is *A Book of Curves* by E. H. Lockwood (Cambridge University Press).

60 A lover's ultimatum

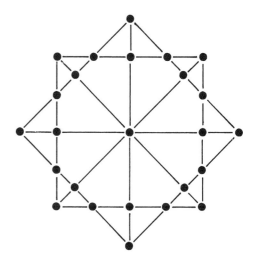

61 Only four lines

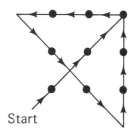

Now try connecting 16 dots in a 4 x 4 array by using six straight lines without lifting your pencil from the paper.

62 How fast can you cycle?

No matter how fast she goes down the hill she cannot average 40 km per hour. To do this she must cycle the 10 kilometres from A to C in a quarter of an hour, but she has already taken a quarter of a hour to climb up to B.

63 The bob-sleigh run

Contrary to what one might think the path is not a straight line from S to V. The path of quickest descent is in fact part of a cycloid and may even be uphill for part of its length. The cycloid is the path traced out by a point on the rim of a wheel as it rolls along a straight line.

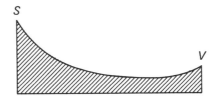

To draw a cycloid fasten to a table a metre rule on top of a piece of paper. Roll a circular object (a tin lid, saucer) along the rule without slipping and trace out the path of a point on the object's edge. You can make a very effective demonstration that this is the path of quickest descent by making two runners, one shaped like part of an inverted cycloid and the other a straight line, out of plywood or a plastic curtain runner down which you simultaneously roll two marbles.

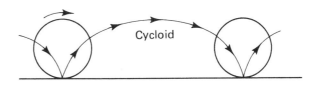

See also *Machines, Mechanisms and Mathematics* by A. B. Bolt and J. E. Hiscocks (Chatto and Windus), or *Riddles in Mathematics* by E. P. Northrop (Pelican).

64 Know your vowels

To make up your own puzzle start with a square and first see how to divide it into pentomines. Then letter it or put some motifs to suit.

E	A	I	O	I
U	E	U	E	O
O	I	A	O	A
I	U	E	A	I
A	O	U	E	U

65 Games on a pegboard for one to play

Pegboard games are of long standing but perhaps underrated because they look deceptively simple.

The smallest number of moves in 'Leapfrog' is fifteen.

Number the holes 1 to 7 from left to right then a solution in fifteen moves is as follows where the number corresponds to the empty hole at each stage:

3   5   6   4   2   1   3   5   7   6   4   2   3   5   4

The strategy is to maximise the number of leaps and in this solution there are nine.

With x black pegs and y red pegs to change ends then the solution can be achieved in $xy + x + y$ moves where xy is the number of leaps.

The games described here and many others are analysed in *Mathematical Recreations and Essays* by W. W. Rouse Ball (Macmillan) while readable references on solitaire problems are *Winning Ways* vol 2 by E. R. Berlekamp, J. H. Conway and R. K. Guy (Academic Press), and *Further Mathematical Diversions* by Martin Gardner (Pelican).

66 Two of a kind

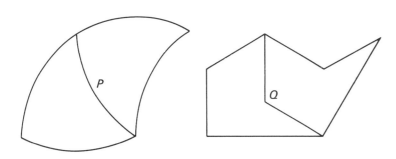

67 Colouring a cube

The smallest number of colours is three, as the three faces meeting at a corner of the cube all have to be different, but if opposite faces are the same colour then no adjacent faces are the same.

With four colours A, B, C and D available then there are four ways of choosing three at a time namely ABC, ABD, ACD and BCD and with each choice only one way of colouring the cube. All other ways must come from using all four colours. It is not easy to sort out the possibilities without a model cube (lumps of sugar can be very helpful here) but to start with note that three faces cannot be coloured the same colour without two adjacent faces being the same. There are thus six faces to be coloured using all four colours which means that two colours must be used twice and two colours once each. This leads to the six solutions indicated by the nets shown here.

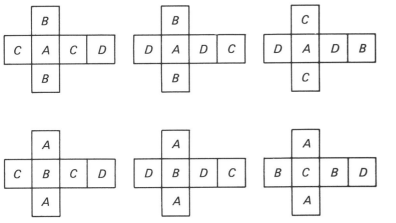

In each case the two colours which occur once must be on opposite faces.

These six solutions with the four earlier solutions using only three colours at a time give a total of ten distinct ways of colouring the cube.

68 Problems of single line working

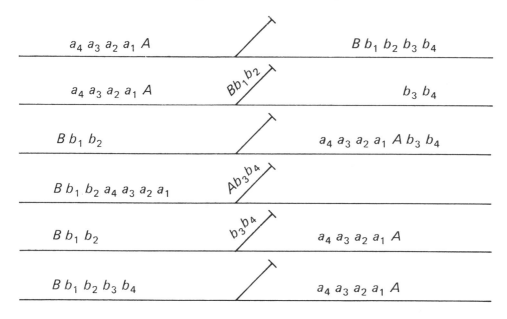

69 Two at a time

Put 7 on 10, 5 on 2, 3 on 8, 1 on 4, 9 on 6.

70 Heads and tails

Initially		H	T	H	T	H	T	H	T
First move	T	H	H	T	H	T	H			T
Second move	T	H	H	T			H	H	T	T
Third move	T			T	H	H	H	H	T	T
Fourth move	T	T	T	T	H	H	H			

71 Square a Greek cross

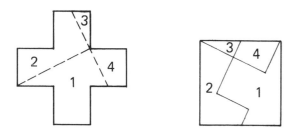

72 The fuel delivery

Depot P I H O N M D E F G S R Q C B L K J A depot

73 Fair shares

Fill 5 from 8. Fill 3 from 5 leaving 2 in 5. Empty 3 into 8.
Pour 2 from 5 into 3. Fill 5 from 8.
Pour from 5 into 3 until full leaving 4 in 5.
Empty 3 into 8 making 4 in 8 also.

74 Coin magic

Moving clockwise around the square pick up the coin in the
middle of each side and place on top of the next corner coin.
The result is a square with a pile of two coins at each of its
vertices so four coins on each side.
   It's easy when you know how!

75 The persistent frog

28 days

76 Tidy that bookshelf!

The number of interchanges required depends on how
muddled the books are, and a systematic way of analysing
this is as follows. First put the required arrangement of the
books above the given arrangement:

Required order	1	2	3	4	5	6	7	8	9
Given order	6	5	7	1	8	9	3	2	4

It then becomes clear that books 3 and 7 are in each others'
positions so that a simple interchange of these, represented
by (37), puts them right.
   None of the other books are so simply displaced. On
inspection we see that

           6 is in the 1 position
           1 is in the 4 position
           4 is in the 9 position
   and   9 is in the 6 position.

so these four books need only be interchanged among
themselves. Their relative positions can be denoted by
(6149) and they can be put into their correct places by a
minimum of three interchanges such as (49) followed by
(14) followed by (61).

The remaining three books' relative positions can be similarly denoted by (528) as

5 is in the position of 2
2 is in the position of 8
and 8 is in the position of 5.

These can then be put in their right positions by the interchange (28) followed by the interchange (52).

Thus the encyclopaedias illustrated could be put into their correct order by the following interchanges

(37) (49) (14) (61) (28) (52)

The solution is not unique but six interchanges is the minimum number of moves from the position given.

Applying the same approach to the second arrangement given

Required order	1	2	3	4	5	6	7	8	9
Given order		4	5	7	6	8	1	9	2	3

we can describe the muddle as

(416) (528) (739)

and this could be put right by a sequence of six interchanges such as

(16) (41) (28) (52) (39) (73).

Now find the minimum number of interchanges to tidy up the order 2 3 5 9 4 1 8 6 7.

77 Cutting up a circle

The number sequence suggests 32 as the solution. In fact the answer is only 31. This is a good example to show that you cannot predict the next number of a sequence with any certainty unless you have more evidence.

For those who understand combinations, the number of pieces produced by n points is given by

$$^{n}C_4 + {}^{n}C_2 + 1$$

78 Square relations

This is a good exercise for using a calculator. One approach is to form a table giving

$$n \quad n^2 \quad n^2 - 1 \quad \tfrac{1}{2}(n^2 - 1)$$

and a solution is found when a number in the $n^2 - 1$ column is repeated somewhere in the $\tfrac{1}{2}(n^2 - 1)$ column.

The solution to this puzzle is 840 as

$$840 + 1 = \;\; 841 = 29^2$$
$$\text{and } (840 \times 2) + 1 = 1681 = 41^2$$

79 The numerate gardener

As in the last puzzle you will need a table of square numbers. The problem is to find whole number solutions to

$$a^2 + b^2 = c^2 + d^2$$

The first solution is

$$6^2 + 7^2 = 2^2 + 9^2 \; = 85$$

Other possible solutions are

$$8^2 + 11^2 = 4^2 + 13^2 = 185$$

$$\text{and } 15^2 + 20^2 = 7^2 + 24^2 = 625$$

80 Magic triangles

Solve these by intelligent use of 'trial and error'.

With 1, 2, 3, 4, 5, 6, the four possibilities are

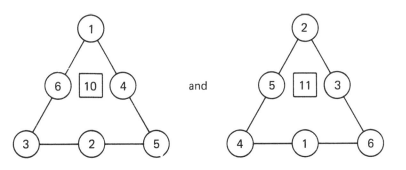

and

105

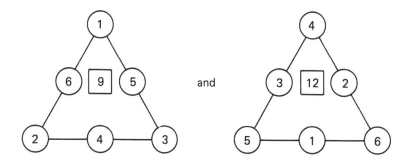

and

Notice how the solutions occur in pairs where the numbers
at the vertices of the triangles change places with the numbers
in the middle of the opposite sides.

With 1, 2, 3, 5, 6, 7 the solutions are

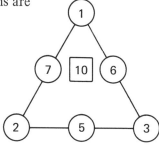

and

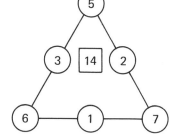

which are closely related to the last two above. How?

With 1, 2, 3, 4, 6, 7, the solutions are

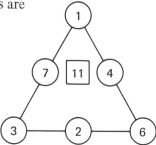

and

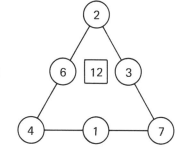

81 Number patterns

1 If the digit is *d* the answer is *ddd ddd ddd*. This is because
12 345 679 = 111 111 111 ÷ 9.

2 If the digit is *d* the answer is *ddd ddd*. In this case 15 873
= 111 111 ÷ 7

3 143 × 7 = 1001 so 143 × *d* × 7 = 1001 × *d* = *d*00*d*.

4 There are probably several logical explanations for each of
these:

(i)   1234 = 1111 + 111 + 11 + 1 + 0

    (1111 × 9) + 1 = 10 000
    (111 × 9) + 1 = 1 000
    (11 × 9) + 1 =   100
    (1 × 9) + 1 =   10
    (0 × 9) + 1 =   1

    (1234 × 9) + 5 = 11 111

This example should show why the pattern occurs.

(ii)
    66 × 67 = 2 × 3 × 11 × 67
            = 22 × 201
            = 4422

    666 × 67 = 2 × 3 × 111 × 67
             = 222 × 2001
             = 444222

and so on.

82 Surprising subtractions

The surprising fact is that no matter what four digits you
start with the end point is 6174. Here is a longer chain.

(i)	7432	(ii)	8550	(iii)	9972	(iv)	7731
−	2347	−	558	−	2799	−	1377
	5085		7992		7173		6354

(v)	6543	(vi)	8730	(vii)	8532	(viii)	7641
−	3456	−	378	−	2358	−	1467
	3087		8352		6174		6174

The author has found chains of eight subtractions needed
before 6174 occurs but he would be interested to hear from
anyone who finds a longer chain.

This activity is best investigated with a calculator, it is a
good idea to jot down the answer to your subtraction at each
stage for if a long chain occurs you will have forgotten the
starting point by the time 6174 occurs.

Try a similar process on five digits or longer numbers.

83 How large a number can you get?

Put the digits in decreasing order:

$$9 \quad 7 \quad 5 \quad 4 \quad 3 \quad 2$$

Then for the largest sum it is only necessary to take the first two digits for the hundreds, the next two digits for the tens, and the last two digits for the units. This gives four possible pairs:

$$\begin{array}{r} 953 \\ +\ 742 \\ \hline 1\ 695 \end{array} \qquad \begin{array}{r} 943 \\ +\ 752 \\ \hline 1\ 695 \end{array} \qquad \begin{array}{r} 952 \\ +\ 743 \\ \hline 1\ 695 \end{array} \qquad \begin{array}{r} 942 \\ +\ 753 \\ \hline 1\ 695 \end{array}$$

However the maximum product is found by taking the pair of numbers from the four here which are closest together, in this case

$$942 \times 753 = 709\ 326$$

One way to understand this is to imagine the four pairs above as representing the sides of a rectangle.

As the sum of each pair is the same the rectangles will all have the same perimeter. The products of the numbers then correspond to the areas of the rectangles and for rectangles of equal perimeter the shape nearest to a square will have the largest area.

84 Four 4s

This is an activity well worth spending time on. As a school activity it is interesting to put the results on the wall and encourage alternative expressions over a period of say a week. Numbers which prove difficult to express vary from person to person but there are one or two intrinsically difficult ones. Feel pleased if you find 95 or more correctly!

$$71 = \frac{4! + 4 \cdot 4}{\cdot 4} \qquad 73 = \frac{\sqrt[\cdot 4]{4} + \dot{\cdot}4}{\cdot 4} \qquad \left[\text{NB } \sqrt[\cdot 4]{4} = 4^{5/2} = 2^5 = 32 \right]$$

$$85 = \frac{4!}{\dot{\cdot}4 \times \sqrt{\cdot 4}} + 4 \qquad 89 = \frac{4! + \sqrt{4}}{\cdot 4} + 4!$$

85 What was the sum?

$$13 \div 29 = 0.4482758 \text{ on a calculator}$$

These questions are easy to set!

86 Calculator words

ShELL.OIL

A calculator never tells LIES.

LESLIE went fishing off LOOE on a LILO for SOLE but only caught some EELS.

BILL decided to SELL hIS walking ShOES because hE had a LOOSE hEEL in one and a hOLE in the other. They hurt like hELL and made him feel quite ILL.

ESSO.

Calculator digit	0	1	2	3	4	5	6	7	8	9
Letter equivalent	O	I or I	Z	E	h	S	g	L	B	b

87 A calculator crossword

	H			L	I	E
G	O	O	S	E		L
	L		E	G	G	S
B	E	L	L			I
I	S		L	O	B	E
B		I			E	
L	E	S	L	I	E	
E			O		S	O

88 A mining bonanza

This is an interesting puzzle for a group of people to do together to see who can find the most profitable route. The idea for this came from an article in the *Mathematical Gazette* no. 418 and in turn came from a sales promotion gimmick by an Australian detergent manufacturer. It has proved particularly motivating in a competitive situation but so far no-one has found the best solution without using a computer. This is probably because the best route,

28 74 45 83 57 72 52 73 41 70 44 81 56

which gives a profit of £776 million, does not visit any of the eleven squares with profits of more than £83 million.

Using this array of numbers it is easy to pose similar but different puzzles. For example, what is the shortest route which would visit all the squares with a profit of at least £80 million?

89 Hundreds, tens and units

The final answer is always 1089 unless the first number chosen has its hundred's digit equal to its unit's digit such as 525 for then the first subtraction yields zero.

90 Magic circles

The possible solutions all depend on the fact that $1+6 = 2+5 = 3+4 = 7$. In each case the pair of squares at the intersection of two circles must contain a pair of numbers which add up to 7. The magic number for each circle is then 14.

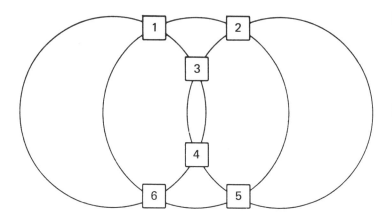

To find another set of six numbers which could be used to form a set of magic circles decide on a number N and find three pairs of numbers $(a, b), (c, d), (e, f)$ whose sum is N. For example, if $N = 15$, then the three pairs of numbers could be

$$(5, 10) \quad (7, 8) \quad (2, 13)$$

A solution would then be

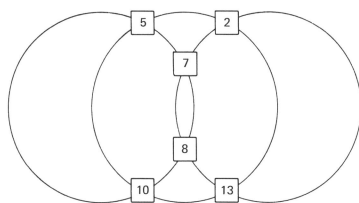

where $2N = 30$ is the magic number.

The solution to the four-circle puzzle depends on the fact that $1 + 12 = 2 + 11 = 3 + 10 = 4 + 9 = 5 + 8 = 6 + 7 = 13$.

Any pair of circles intersect in only two points so put a pair of numbers at these two points which add up to 13. In this way it is easy to find a solution. One is given here.

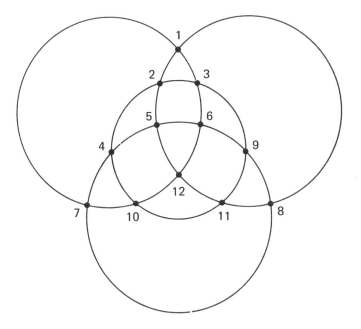

$$1 + 2 + 5 + 12 + 11 + 8 = 39$$
$$2 + 3 + 9 + 11 + 10 + 4 = 39$$
$$1 + 3 + 6 + 12 + 10 + 7 = 39$$
$$7 + 4 + 5 + 6 + 9 + 8 \quad = 39$$

91 Prelude to a marathon

Several solutions, but all involve a carry. One solution is

```
   154
+ 782
─────
   936
```

and others can be obtained from it by interchanging suitable pairs of numbers such as

```
   152          215          278
+ 784        + 478        + 415
─────        ─────        ─────
   936          693          693
```

How many possible solutions are there?

92 Find the digits

```
   7641
− 1467
─────
   6174
```

See puzzle 82, Surprising subtractions.

Many sets of four letters can be permuted to form a variety of words as, for example,

EVIL   LIVE   VILE   VEIL   LEVI,

but not many can be found where three of the words fit the above number pattern exactly. One further example is

```
  ABLE
- ELBA
───────
  BEAL
```

93   Dr Numerati's telephone number

$$37 \times 41 \times 43 = 65\,231$$

so Dr Numerati lived in number 41, and 65231 was her telephone number.

94   Make a century

Here are four solutions.

$$123 - 4 - 5 - 6 - 7 + 8 - 9 = 100$$
$$123 - 45 - 67 + 89 \qquad\quad = 100$$
$$[1 \times (2+3) \times 4 \times 5] + 6 - 7 - 8 + 9 = 100$$
$$(1 \times 2 \times 3) - (4 \times 5) + (6 \times 7) + (8 \times 9) = 100$$

95   Number wheels

The bottom spoke has all its numbers present and totals 23. The number in the centre can now be found as $23 - 15 - 2 = 6$ and the rest rapidly follow.

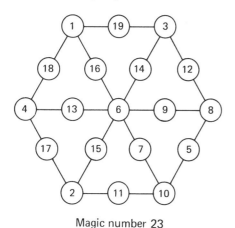

Magic number 23

Magic number 22

96 Some calculator challenges

Because a calculator takes the drudgery out of arithmetic challenges like the ones here become relatively easy.

(i) 237×238 First find $\sqrt{(56\,406)}$.

(ii) Intelligent use of trial and error should soon give
      $69 \times 71 \times 73 = 357\,406$

(iii) $26^2 + 27^2 = 1405$

(iv) The intention here is to try different numbers and gradually get closer to the actual length.

      $5 \times 5 \times 5 = 125$ and $6 \times 6 \times 6 = 216$

      so the required length will be somewhere between 5 and 6 but nearer to 6.

Try	5·9	:	$5·9 \times 5·9 \times 5·9$	=	205·379
Next	5·8	:	$5·8 \times 5·8 \times 5·8$	=	195·112
	5·85	:	$5·85 \times 5·85 \times 5·85$	=	200·201 62
	5·845	:	$5·845^3$	=	199·688 72
	5·848	:	$5·848^3$	=	199·996 36
	5·848 1	:	$5·848\,1^3$	=	200·006 61
	5·848 04	:	$5·848\,04^3$	=	200·000 45
	5·848 035	:	$5·848\,035^3$	=	199·999 94

On a variety of calculators

   $5·848\,035\,5^3 = 200$

This is not necessarily the *exact* answer, though within the accuracy of the calculator it is.

97 Division patterns

Because in the past without a calculator we usually only carried out a division process for say 4 significant figures it was only when dividing by numbers like 3 and 11 which give short repeating patterns that we were aware of the possibility of a recurring decimal. The fact that virtually all division sums if continued far enough lead to a repeating pattern probably comes as a surprise.

1 With division by 7 the pattern will always settle down to a recurring sequence of six digits.

$$\frac{8}{7} = 1\tfrac{1}{7} = 1·142857$$

$$\frac{9}{7} = 1\tfrac{2}{7} = 1·285714$$

$$\frac{16}{7} = 2\tfrac{2}{7} = 2·285714$$

$$\frac{1}{7} = 0·142857\ 142857 \ldots$$

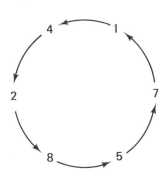

To see that division by a number such as 64 or 320 always terminates is probably best seen with an example.

Consider $\dfrac{73}{64} = \dfrac{73}{2^6} = \dfrac{73 \times 5^6}{2^6 \times 5^6} = \dfrac{1140625}{1000000} = 1\cdot140625$

If the number is not made up of a power of 2 and a power of 5 then it cannot be converted into a power of 10 as in the example here.

When dividing by a number such as 31, for example, then there are 30 possible remainders namely 1, 2, . . . , 30 which could all occur before one is repeated so to study repeating sequences in the quotient it is really a case of studying the sequence of remainders. There is a nice tie-up here with modulo arithmetic groups for anyone interested.

2 For division by 17 the sequence of digits is

2 9 4 1 1 7 6 4 7 0 5 8 8 2 3 5

$\dfrac{5}{17} = 0\cdot2\,9\,4\,1\,1\,7\,6\,4\,7\,0\,5\,8\,8\,2\,3\,5\,2\,9\,4\,1$

$\dfrac{6}{17} = 0\cdot3\,5\,2\,9\,4\,1\,1\,7\,6\,4\,7\,0\,5\,8\,8\,2\,3\,5\,2\,9$

$\dfrac{7}{17} = 0\cdot4\,1\,1\,7\,6\,4\,7\,0\,5\,8\,8\,2\,3\,5\,2\,9\,4\,1\,1\,7$

3 For division by 19 the sequence of digits is

3 6 8 4 2 1 0 5 2 6 3 1 5 7 8 9 4 7

4 Division by 11 always leads to a sequence of two digits which can be

09	18	27	36	45
90	81	72	63	54

5 Division by 13 leads to one of two six-digit sequences

0 7 6 9 2 3   or   1 5 3 8 4 6

98 Some named numbers

Palindromic numbers

The smallest palindromic prime is 11 and the smallest palindromic square is 121. There are only two other palindromic squares less than 1000:

$$484 = 22^2 \quad \text{and} \quad 676 = 26^2$$

The palindromic primes between 100 and 200 are

$$101 \quad 131 \quad 151 \quad 181 \quad 191$$

Any palindromic number : between 400 and 500 would have to end in 4 so would be an even number; between 500 and 600 would have to end in 5 so would have 5 as a factor; between 600 and 700 would have to end in 6 so would be even. In fact there are no palindromic primes between 383 and 727. The common factor is 11.

99 Magic stars

The magic number is 40 in each case.

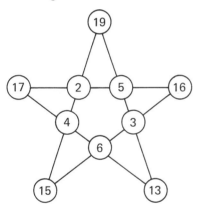
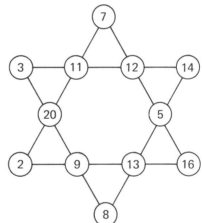

They may be solved by intelligent use of trial and error or analytically using simultaneous linear equations.

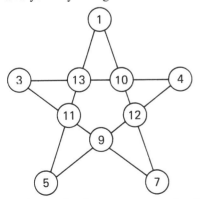
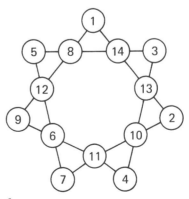

A good reference on magic stars is *Magic Squares and Cubes* by W. S. Andrews (Dover).

100 Safety first

Both the puzzles here are in general circulation but if you have not met them before they offer a satisfactory challenge to your powers of reasoning. The key is to start from the left-hand end where the possible values of D (or M) are strictly limited.

(a)   9 6 2 3 3
   + 6 2 5 1 3
    1 5 8 7 4 6

(b)   9 5 6 7
   + 1 0 8 5
    1 0 6 5 2

Other similar problems to try are

    T H R E E
+ T H R E E
      F O U R
───────
E L E V E N

    T H I S
+   I S
    V E R Y
───────
   E A S Y

  S A N T A
− C L A U S
───────
   X M A S

  S P E N D
− M O R E
───────
  M O N E Y

101 The gambler's secret strategy

If the opponent chooses red the gambler chooses blue.
If the opponent chooses blue the gambler chooses yellow.
If the opponent chooses yellow the gambler chooses red.

In each case the gambler has a chance of winning, on average, five rolls of dice out of every nine rolls.

This is a fascinating situation. The numbers on the faces of each dice total the same and no single dice is better than both the others. To see why the blue dice is superior to the red dice consider the possible ways in which the two dice could land:

Score on red dice	Possible score on blue dice		
2	$\underline{3}$	$\underline{5}$	$\underline{7}$
4	3	$\underline{5}$	$\underline{7}$
9	3	5	7

The times when blue has a larger score have been underlined and of the nine possible combinations, each of which are equally likely, blue comes out above red on five occasions. Similarly it can be shown why yellow is superior to blue and red superior to yellow.

102 The transportation problem

	P	Q	R	S
A	4			5
B	1	5		
C	3		7	

or

	P	Q	R	S
A		4		5
B	5	1		
C	3		7	

Both these allocations lead to a distance of 67 miles. This problem is one of a general type which has a specific method of solution although here it was expected to be done by intelligent use of trial and error.

For further reading on this type of problem read, for example, *An Introduction to Linear Programming and the Theory of Games* by S. Vajda (Methuen/Wiley) or *Mathematics in Management* by A. Battersby (Pelican).

103 Further number patterns

1 $x^2 - y^2 = (x + y)(x - y)$
In this case $x - y = 1$ so $x^2 - y^2 = x + y$.

2 If the number being squared is n then the two other numbers being multiplied together are $n - 1$ and $n + 1$.
Now $(n - 1)(n + 1) = n^2 - 1$
so the product is always 1 less than n^2.

3 With powers of 3 the last digit repeats the cycle 3, 9, 7, 1.
Powers of 2 give the sequence 2, 4, 8, 6.
Powers of 4 give the sequence 4, 6.
Powers of 5 and 6 just give 5 and 6.
Powers of 7 give the sequence 7, 9, 3, 1.
Powers of 8 give the sequence 8, 4, 2, 6.
Powers of 9 give the sequence 9, 1.
Note the close connection between the patterns of 3 and 7 and between those of 2 and 8.

4 The nth line consists of n consecutive odd numbers ending in the $\frac{1}{2}n(n + 1)$th odd number and their sum is equal to n^3.

5 The sum of the cubes of the first n numbers is equal to the square of the sum of the first n numbers. For example

$$1^3 + 2^3 + 3^3 + 4^3 = (1 + 2 + 3 + 4)^2$$

104 Pythagorean triads

The main triads with numbers less than 50 are

3	4	5
5	12	13
7	24	25
8	15	17
9	40	41
12	35	37
20	21	29

Each give triangle area 210. (for last two rows)

Others are also possible as multiples of these such as

6 8 10 or 15 36 39 or 16 30 34

Because of the identity

$$(m^2 - n^2)^2 + (2mn)^2 = (m^2 + n^2)^2$$

new Pythagorean triads can be easily found by giving whole number values to m and n and then calculating the numbers

$$m^2 - n^2 \quad 2mn \quad m^2 + n^2$$

Some three-dimensional examples are

2	3	6	7
1	4	8	9
3	16	24	29

105 Intriguing multiplications

138 × 42 = 5796	198 × 27 = 5346
483 × 12 = 5796	297 × 18 = 5346
186 × 39 = 7254	1738 × 4 = 6952
157 × 28 = 4396	1963 × 4 = 7852

Also   51 249 876 × 3 = 153 749 628
and   32 547 891 × 6 = 195 287 346

A good reference on this and many fascinating number relations is *Recreations in the Theory of Numbers* by A. H. Beiler (Dover).

106 A magic diamond

The numbers will be of the form

$$a = x \qquad b = 5 + x$$
$$c = 3 + x \qquad d = 11 + x$$

where x is any number and the total along each line will then be $20 + 2x$.

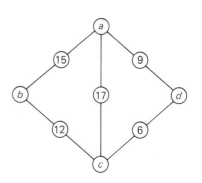

For example, if $x = 1$, then $a = 1, b = 6, c = 4, d = 12$ and each line total will be 22.

118

107 Palindromic dates

In a year such as 1982 every month apart from October or December will have a palindromic date on the 28th of the month, for example 28.6.82. In addition 1982 contains the palindromic date 2.8.82, so in all it contains eleven palindromic dates.

We are now in for a lean time however as the only palindromic date in 1983 is 3.8.83 with similar August dates up to 9.8.89.

The closest palindromic dates will be obtained by finding the right juxtaposition of dates with a two-digit day and a single-digit day in the same or adjacent months. Two good solutions are

> 1.2.21 followed by 12.2.21
> and 22.1.22 followed by 2.2.22

with gaps of eleven days, but the best solution would seem to be

> 29.8.92 followed by 2.9.92

with a gap of only four days.

108 'Mind reading' number cards

The other four cards are

2	3	6	7
10	11	14	15
18	19	22	23
26	27	30	31

4	5	6	7
12	13	14	15
20	21	22	23
28	29	30	31

Based on the binary representation of number, these cards are sometimes found in Christmas crackers. What is certain is that they create much interest even when both participants know how the cards work.

8	9	10	11
12	13	14	15
24	25	26	27
28	29	30	31

16	17	18	19
20	21	22	23
24	25	26	27
28	29	30	31

109 3 × 3 magic squares

6	1	8
7	5	3
2	9	4

(b)

9	2	10
8	7	6
4	12	5

(c)

14	3	10
5	9	13
8	15	4

(d)

11	1	12
9	8	7
4	15	5

(e)

When using the method given for generating new magic squares some care should be made in choosing the differences so that all the numbers generated are different. The method works for any numbers as the following shows.

Let a be the first number and p and q the differences. The numbers generated and the resulting magic square are

a	$a + p$	$a + 2p$
$a + q$	$a + p + q$	$a + 2p + q$
$a + 2q$	$a + p + 2q$	$a + 2p + 2q$

$a + p + 2q$	a	$a + 2p + q$
$a + 2p$	$a + p + q$	$a + 2q$
$a + q$	$a + 2p + 2q$	$a + p$

The magic number is $3(a + p + q)$ which shows that for a 3 × 3 magic square of whole numbers the magic number is always a multiple of 3.

Can you find a, p and q so that all the numbers in the square are prime?

110 4 × 4 and higher order magic squares

Other sets of four numbers which total 34 in Dürer's magic square are

```
 3   2  15  14          5   9   8  12
10  11   6   7          2  12  15   5
16   3  10   5          2  13  11   8
 9   6   4  15          7  12  14   1
 9   4  13   8         16   5  12   1
16   3  14   1          2  13   4  15
 3  10   7  14          6  15   2  11
 5  10   7  12          9   6  11   8
```

In the Nasik magic square most of the symmetries of the Dürer square exist but in addition there are diagonal patterns such as

15	14	2	3
10	4	7	13
14	9	3	8

10	11	7	6
11	16	6	1
15	5	2	12

The fullest reference on magic squares is probably *Magic Squares and Cubes* by W. S. Andrews (Dover), but there is much of interest in *Mathematical Recreations and Essays* by W. W. Rouse Ball (Macmillan), and in *Amusements in Mathematics* by H. E. Dudeney (Dover).

111 A magic cube

Middle layer

23	3	16
7	14	21
12	25	5

Bottom layer

18	22	2
20	9	13
4	11	27

For much more on magic cubes see *Magic Squares and Cubes* by W. S. Andrews.

112 A question of balance

Compare 9 balls with 9 balls and leave 9 in the box. If the scales balance then the heavy ball is in the box, if not then the 9 balls which go down contains the heavy ball. Either way, after one balance the faulty ball has been narrowed down to a set of 9. Divide this set of 9 into three sets of 3 After this you will have narrowed down the faulty ball to 3 and one more balance sorts it out.

A similar but much harder problem is to find the odd ball from 13 in three balances if all you know is that the odd ball has a different weight to the other 12.

113 Further calculator challenges

(i) Do the division, subtract the whole number part of the quotient, and multiply the resulting decimal number by 729.

One calculator gave

$$89\,328 \div 729 = 122.534\,97$$

$$0.534\,97 \times 729 = 389.993\,13$$

Because of the limitations in the capacity of a calculator there are errors in the last few digits but the remainder can be confidently given as the nearest whole number, 390.

Check by seeing that $(729 \times 122) + 390 = 89\,328$

Alternatively from the initial division the remainder can be found as

$$89\,328 - (729 \times 122) = 390$$

thus avoiding the need to round off.

(ii) As $\alpha^3 = 200$ can be written as

$$\alpha^2 = \frac{200}{\alpha}$$

from which $\alpha = \sqrt{\left(\dfrac{200}{\alpha}\right)}$

it follows that if x is an approximation to the cube root of 200 then $\sqrt{(200/x)}$ is a better approximation. For example if $x_1 = 6$ is taken as the first approximation to $\sqrt[3]{200}$ then take

$$x_2 = \sqrt{\frac{200}{6}} \doteqdot 5.7735$$

$$x_3 = \sqrt{\frac{200}{5.7735}} \doteqdot 5.885\,66$$

$$x_4 = \sqrt{\frac{200}{5.885\,66}} \doteqdot 5.829\,31$$

$$x_5 = \sqrt{\frac{200}{5.829\,31}} \doteqdot 5.857\,42 \text{ etc.}$$

This method converges automatically to the required number. It may not be as quick as a skilled operator using trial and error but it would be easy to program.

(iii) What is infinity on your calculator!

Start with a string of 9s and then keep reducing until you get other than 0 for an answer.

114 A weighing problem

The weights are 1 kg, 3 kg, 9 kg and 27 kg. By putting the weights on either scale pan then all the weights from 1 to 40 can be achieved. For example

$$11 = 9 + 3 - 1 \qquad 20 = 27 + 3 - 9 - 1$$

115   Similar rectangles

The lengths must be in the ratio of $\sqrt{2} : 1$ as

$$\frac{x}{1} = \frac{1}{x/2}$$

giving $\qquad x^2 = 2$

from which $\qquad x = \sqrt{2}$

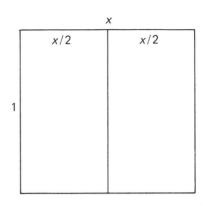

116   Designing a new dartboard

The solution shown here maximises the sum of the differences between adjacent numbers. Here there are

$$\begin{array}{rl} & 10 \text{ gaps of } 10 \\ & 9 \text{ gaps of } 9 \\ \text{and} & 1 \text{ gap of } 19 \end{array}$$

giving a total of 200.

In general, if n is an even number, the numbers 1, 2, 3, . . . , n can be placed around a circle so that the sum of the gaps is $\frac{1}{2}n^2$.

What arrangement of the numbers would minimise the sum of the differences?

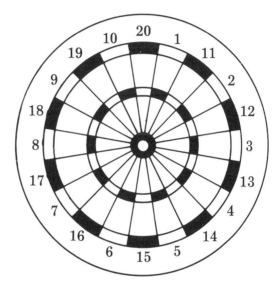

117   The only magic hexagon

This magic hexagon was first discovered by an Englishman, T. Vickers, who published it in the December 1958 *Mathematical Gazette*.

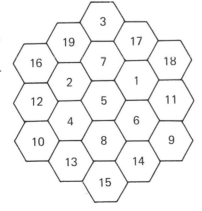

118 Nim

The game of Nim is analysed in *Mathematical Recreations and Essays* by W. W. Rouse Ball (Macmillan) and there is an interesting chapter in *We Built our Own Computers* by A. B. Bolt (Cambridge University Press) describing a machine which could play the game.

The game is interesting because every position of the game can be classified as 'safe' or 'unsafe'.

From a safe position a player can only create an unsafe position no matter how many counters he moves. However from an unsafe position it is possible to move to either a safe or an unsafe position. Thus a player who has analysed the game can always move from an unsafe position to a safe position and beat his opponent.

There are many more unsafe positions than safe positions but to proceed it is necessary to find out how to decide which are which.

Take the example given in the description of the game. First convert the number of counters in each heap into binary and add up the digits in each column without resorting to carry.

	Binary form
7	111
9	1001
6	110
Digit sum	1222

For a safe position the digit sum for each column must be an even number. Hence the position here is unsafe.

To move to a safe position the second heap could be reduced to 1

then 7	111	is a safe position
1	1	
6	110	
	222	

Why is this the only safe move from this position? Other safe positions are, for example, (2, 4, 6)   (2, 5, 7)   (1, 2, 3)   (7, 10, 13).

Playing against an uninitiated player a player who can use the strategy described here should win nine times out of ten but he cannot win if the starting position is unsafe and his opponent moves to a safe move from it and on every subsequent move. Faced with a safe position the best strategy is to remove just one counter (i.e. do as little as possible) in the hope that your opponent's next move will be to an unsafe position.

119 Triangulating a square

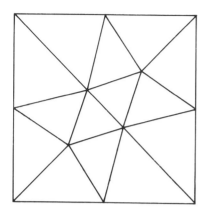

The author had convinced himself that it was not possible to triangulate a square with acute angled triangles until sent the adjoining solution by Dr Hugh L. Porteous of Sheffield City Polytechnic. Note its symmetry about the two diagonals.

120 Who is 'it'?

Start at a and keep counting on 13 crossing out the letter you reach. The result will be that g is left in at the end. Thus to leave c last, which is opposite g, start at e.

121 Find the cards on the table

The solution is as shown. It can be deduced in the following way.

Suppose that the face value of four adjacent cards is a, b, c, d. Then

$$b + c + d = a + b + c$$
$$\text{or} \quad b + c + d = a + b + c + 1$$
$$\text{or} \quad b + c + d = a + b + c - 1.$$

The first of these alternatives leads to $a = d$ which is not possible while the others give $d = a + 1$ or $d = a - 1$. Taking $d = a + 1$ (the other alternative leads to the same final solution) we have four adjacent cards with face values of

$$a \quad b \quad c \quad a + 1$$

Using the same argument above to generate the face value of the next card we find it has to be $b - 1$, the next $c + 1$ and the card after that has to be a; so we are back to where we started with only the six cards

$$a \quad b \quad c \quad a + 1 \quad b - 1 \quad c + 1$$

in that order around the circle. $(a, a + 1)$, $(b, b - 1)$ and $(c, c + 1)$ are consecutive pairs of numbers and as 2, 5, 6 and 10 are given it follows that the missing cards are 3 and 9.

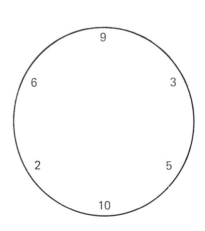

122 Dividing the inheritance

No point exists inside the ranch from which lines can be
drawn to the corners to form four triangles of equal area.
It is only possible for a quadrilateral to be divided up in
this way when the diagonal (AC) of the quadrilateral
bisects its area, then the mid-point M of the diagonal is
the required point.

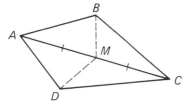

123 The end of the world!

Surprising as it may seem the first day of a century can
never occur on a Sunday, a Tuesday or a Thursday. In
1582 to improve the accuracy of the calendar, Pope Gregory
XIII decreed that instead of every fourth year being a leap
year an exception would be made for centurial years not
divisible by 400. Thus 2000 is a leap year but the years
2100, 2200 and 2300 would not be even though they are
divisible by 4.

To see what effect this has on century days consider
the number of days from January 1st on one century day
to January 1st in the next century. There are 100 years
which would normally contain 25 leap years and hence
36 525 days which is equivalent to 5217 weeks and 6 days.
Thus from one century day to the next, without Pope
Gregory's adjustment, the weekday would move on by 6.
However this only happens when a century day follows on
from a century divisible by 400. When this is not the case,
there will only be 24 leap years in the intervening century
so the day will only move on by 5. A little calculation will
soon show that the century day in the year 2000 is Saturday.
Then

Year	2000	2100	2200	2300	2400	2500	...
Century day	Sat	Fri	Wed	Mon	Sat	Fri	...
		+6	+5	+5	+5	+6	

This cycle of events continues so that the century day never
falls on a Sunday, Tuesday or Thursday.

The end is not in sight!

124 The sponsored marathon

Each sponsor had agreed to pay

$$(1 + 2 + 4 + 8 + 16 + .. + 2^{25}) \text{ pence.}$$

This series sums to $2^{26} - 1 = 67\,108\,863$ pence. This is £671 089 or the equivalent of £25 811 for every mile run. Let us hope that every person who sponsored this particular runner was a millionaire!

125 The effect of inflation

The formula connecting the rate of inflation $r\%$, the initial price P and the final price P_n after n years of inflation is

$$P_n = (1 + \frac{r}{100})^n P$$

Thus for the house price

$$34\,000 = (1 + \frac{r}{100})^{20} \times 3500$$

Using a calculator gives

$$1 + \frac{r}{100} = 1.120\,393\,4$$

from which the rate of inflation is about 12%.
    Similarly, for the cost of petrol

$$184 = (1 + \frac{r}{100})^{18} \times 33$$

which gives

$$1 + \frac{r}{100} = 1.100\,173\,9$$

from which the rate of inflation is about 10%.
    If these rates of inflation should continue then in the year 2000 the house will cost £294 794 and a gallon of petrol will be 933p.

126 Octogenarian occupations

$$8^3 - 7^3 = 512 - 343 = 169 = 13^2$$

The retired teacher was 87 and his great granddaughter was 13.

127 Tails up!

Only the first of these coin puzzles is impossible.

1 Any move from the starting point of three heads (H^3) leads to a single head and two tails (HT^2) while any move from HT^2 leads to H^3 or HT^2 again, thus only two basic arrangements are possible and the only moves from them are neatly summarised by

2 Possible in four moves. One solution is

H	H	H	H
H*	T	T	T
T	T*	H	H
H	H	H*	T
T	T	T	T*

The asterisk indicates the coin which was not turned over in the move.

You may like to investigate the possible arrangements from five coins when a move consists of turning over any four, etc.

3 Possible in five moves. Label the nine coins $a, b, c, \ldots, i$ as shown. Then one solution consists of the following moves:

(i)   turn $a\,e\,i$
(ii) turn $b\,e\,h$ $a\ \ b\ \ c$
(iii) turn $c\,e\,g$ $d\ \ e\ \ f$
(iv) turn $a\,b\,c$ $g\ \ h\ \ i$
(v)   turn $g\,h\,i$

Which arrangements of head and tail are possible?
Would the puzzle still be possible if the diagonal moves are excluded?

128 Dovetailed

The dovetails are cut at a diagonal, not parallel to the faces of the block as the apprentices had thought.

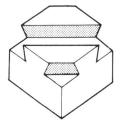
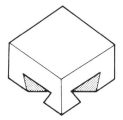

129 More matchstick mindbenders

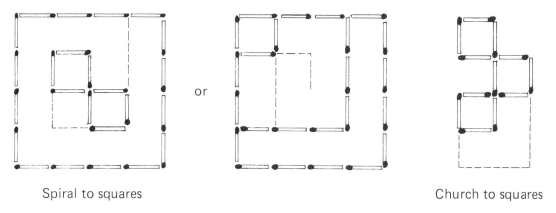

Spiral to squares

or

Church to squares

130 Bridging the river

Try experimenting with a pile of dominoes to represent the sleepers. With three sleepers the best which can be achieved is $3\frac{2}{3}$ metres.

The smallest number of sleepers which will enable the structure to overlap the opposite bank, 5 metres away, is seven.

To understand how the solution is reached consider the sequence of diagrams. With one sleeper it can clearly be pushed out across the river for a distance of 2 metres, to the point at which its centre of mass is immediately over the edge of the bank. With two sleepers, the top sleeper can similarly overlap the bottom sleeper by 2 metres before it tips, and the bottom sleeper remains stable as long as the centre of mass of both sleepers taken together (shown with a cross in the diagram) is at the river's edge. A little thought will show that this gives an extra 1 metre to the overhang giving a total overhang of 3 metres.

When a third sleeper is introduced, the top two sleepers can overhang the bottom one by 3 metres, and the bottom sleeper is arranged so that the combined centre of mass of the three sleepers is at the river's edge. In this case the bottom sleeper protrudes over the river $\frac{2}{3}$ metre.

Each successive sleeper extends the bridge, but by smaller and smaller amounts leading to the following formula for the maximum overhang (d) when n sleepers are used

$$d = 2 \left(1 + \tfrac{1}{2} + \tfrac{1}{3} + \tfrac{1}{4} + \tfrac{1}{5} + \ldots + \frac{1}{n}\right) \text{ metres}$$

When $n = 6$,

$$d = 2\left(1 + \tfrac{1}{2} + \tfrac{1}{3} + \tfrac{1}{4} + \tfrac{1}{5} + \tfrac{1}{6}\right) = 4.9 \text{ metres}$$

which just falls short of the far bank, but when $n = 7$,

$$d = 4.9 + \tfrac{2}{7} \simeq 5.19 \text{ metres}$$

To the mathematician the above formula is fascinating for it indicates that given a sufficient number of sleepers it is theoretically possible to build a structure on one bank which will overlap the far bank no matter how wide the river may be.

Similar problems to this are discussed in *Puzzlemath* by G. Gamow and M. Stern (Macmillan), and *Ingenious Mathematical Problems* by L. A. Graham (Dover).